# ADELE

## DATE DUE

| | | | |
|---|---|---|---|
| Dec. 29, 2016 | | | |
| | | | |
| | | | |
| | | | |
| | | | |
| | | | |
| | | | |
| | | | |
| | | | |
| | | | |
| | | | |

THIS IS A CARLTO

First published in 2(
This edition publish
by Carlton Books L
20 Mortimer Street
London W1T 3JW

Copyright © 2014, :

A CIP catalogue for this book is available from the British Library.

ISBN 978-1-78097-823-9

Printed in Dubai

10 9 8 7 6 5 4 3 2 1

# ADELE

## A Celebration of an Icon and Her Music

Sarah-Louise James

CARLTON BOOKS

# Contents

# 1

# Someone Like Adele

Imagine the scene: 14-year-old Adele Adkins, dressed in her favourite baggy jeans and grunge dog collar necklace – her auburn hair pulled back in a scruffy ponytail – is wiping clean the Formica-topped tables at her aunt's café in North London after another busy Sunday shift. She is listening to the UK Top 40 rundown, humming along to hits from her favourite pop artists, Emma Bunton, Geri Halliwell, Pink, Kylie and Destiny's Child, not thinking beyond the fact that it's school again tomorrow. Had you told this ordinary-looking teen that in 10 years' time not only would she have outstripped sales of albums by her heroines, the Spice Girls, in both the UK and the US, equalled her American idol Beyoncé's record Grammy Award tally for a single night, had Kylie gasping in awe at her singing talent, graced the front cover of the world's most revered fashion bible, and had the small honour of being named the biggest-selling artist of the twenty-first century, she'd have laughed – in that deep, dirty cackle of hers – right in your face.

Back in 2002, London teen Adele had no idea what life had in store. Sure she loved music and singing – but as far as she was concerned she was a thousand times more likely to end up behind a cash register than a microphone. Her live performances started and ended with putting concerts on for her mum's friends in her bedroom. The only time she had seen

▶ Icon: From humble beginnings, Adele has become a modern pop phenomenon. This photograph was taken in February 2011.

her name up in lights had been when her mum had constructed
a makeshift spot-lit stage for her, using a stack of household
lamps. Adele loved to sing at the top of her lungs and knew
she could string more than a few notes together, but she was a
million miles away from believing she could one day be a star,
or anywhere close to harnessing the incredible, soul-stirring
power of the voice we all know and love.

Back then she envisaged her life following the pattern of that
of many of her friends: she would leave school at 16, find a job,
meet someone, have a baby, settle down and carry on trilling
along to other people's records on the radio. Life had other plans
for Adele, however. And so did she. She just didn't know it yet.

Fast-forward a decade and, taking in the odd bump in the
road, Adele's success story is a contemporary fairytale writ large.
The little girl from London is a global megastar and modern-
day icon, celebrated for a voice that can make spines tingle from
a thousand paces, songs that resonate with anyone who has
half a soul and a personality as huge as her now healthy bank
balance. The world-famous artists she once cited as her own
musical inspiration now cite her as theirs. From a scruffy flat in
Tottenham to a multimillion-pound Surrey mansion, her home is
now crammed with awards, while her name dominates the pages
of *Guinness World Records*. And, as big a star in the notoriously
hard-to-crack United States as she is at home in the UK, she has
achieved it all on talent alone.

Let's take a look at how it all began...

# 2

# The Hometown Years

Adele Blue Laurie Adkins's beginnings were humble. She wasn't born into a rock star family or a clan with money and connections. She was born in working-class Tottenham, North London, on Thursday, May 5, 1988, to parents Penny Adkins and Mark Evans. Eighteen-year-old art student Penny and 22-year-old Mark got together in the typical way – their eyes met across a crowded London bar. They chatted, flirted, fell in love, moved in together within months and shortly afterwards announced they were having a baby. It wasn't ideal. Their parents weren't thrilled and Penny had to scrap her plans to go to university.

They may not have planned to start a family so soon but they made the best of it, and when Adele entered the world the couple were besotted with their green-eyed, auburn-haired little girl. Penny and Mark had to work hard to make ends meet, but they had fun, and for the first couple of years, mum, dad, and baby girl formed a strong family unit. Adele might not have been born into the Tottenham equivalent of the Jacksons, but Penny and Mark had a record collection to impress even the snootiest of music critics, and it made its mark on Adele from an early age. You only need look at her distinctive middle name to work out where her dad's musical tastes lay. The Etta (James), Ella (Fitzgerald) Marvin (Gaye)-loving Mark wanted Adele's first

▶ Three-year-old Adele opening presents on Christmas Day 1991 – she received her first guitar just a year later.

name to be Blue, so in love was he with rhythm-and-blues music. He almost got his way. But Penny decided Adele was prettier, so Adele it was. As a baby, Adele's dad would cradle her while playing the classics, and the sounds of Louis Armstrong, Bob Dylan and Nina Simone were often to be heard filtering from the young family home.

While Mark was into the classics, Penny had more contemporary tastes. As befitting her arty soul, she loved rock and indie music, in particular the Cure. And when Adele was just two, she took her to see the band play an open-air concert in nearby Finsbury Park, making little Miss Adkins pretty much the coolest toddler in town.

However harmonious Penny and Mark's relationship had been in the early days, it wasn't meant to be, and the couple split when Adele was just three. Mark left London and returned to his native Wales, and Penny and Adele downsized – moving to a different flat – a pattern that was to repeat itself throughout Adele's early years.

*"I want to be a ballet dancer, no, a saxophone player, no, a weather girl."*

It wasn't easy for single mum Penny and young Adele, but what they lacked in space, money, and the presence of a father figure, they made up for with love. The pair forged a bond so close it became impenetrable. "[We're as] thick as thieves. She's the love of my life," Adele says of Penny. "Of course, it's love/hate sometimes. But mostly love. She doesn't worry about little things. She's never disappointed. You know that parent thing, 'I am not angry, I am disappointed.' Like a bullet. She's not like that. She's honest and open and so supportive.

"I was one of those kids that was like, 'I want to be a ballet dancer, no, a saxophone player, no, a weather girl.' And my mum would run me to all these classes. She has always said, 'Do what you want and if you're happy, I'm happy.'"

Although her dad was not around much while she was

growing up, Adele maintained some sort of relationship with him until she was about eleven. She would visit him in Cardiff during the long summer holidays – sometimes with Penny – and they would go on holidays together, which also gave Adele the chance to spend long stretches of time with her paternal grandparents. During the six weeks off school, she also became close to her half-brother Cameron – her dad's son from his new relationship. Now she says, "Cameron looks like my twin. We're identical, same hair and everything. It's bizarre growing up in a completely different city but then when you see each other, it's as if you've spent every day of your lives together. Straight away I'm bullying him. Straight away he's like … you f**k off. It's amazing, immediate. He's lovely. Really shy, which is the only difference."

Adele's barely there relationship with her dad took a nosedive and never recovered after her beloved granddad John died of cancer. Mark took the loss of his father very badly and began drinking heavily. Soon after John passed away, Mark's best friend died of a heart attack. Finding it difficult to handle his grief, Mark found his dependency on alcohol deepen and turn into a serious addiction. He lost touch with Adele and admits his drinking got so out of hand, he made "Oliver Reed look like a teetotaller." Adele didn't see her father once between the ages of 11 and 14, and Mark has since said it was because he was too ashamed to let her see him that way. "I barely knew my own name let alone my responsibilities. But I did know I didn't want Adele to see me like that. I knew she'd be missing her grandfather as much as I was. She adored him. Yet all I could do was drink. I know I was a rotten father."

The relationship between Adele and her dad had crumbled into nothing. However, in 2011 Mark told his story to the *Sun* newspaper, claiming he wanted to reconnect with her. To say this didn't go down well with Adele is an understatement. She was incensed. "I was actually ready to start a relationship with him," she said. "He's f**king blown it. He will never hear from me again."

She may never have forged a real bond with her dad, but that wasn't the case with her paternal grandparents, who were a huge

▶ A young Adele showing off her fashion chops down on the farm… albeit in a day-glo shell suit.

influence on her. "[My nan was] funny, man. Literally a few hours before she died, she woke up and said, 'I must put my makeup on,'" she remembers. She loved that her paternal grandparents had met when they were 15 and stayed together their entire lives. "Because of that, I always wanted my first boyfriend to be the love of my life," she said. She also adored her granddad for the support he gave Penny. "He just loved my mum and because my dad wasn't in her life, they completely took her over as their daughter," she recalls.

Adele might have been the only child of a single-parent family, but she was never lonely. Growing up in the heart of an extended family, surrounded by cousins, aunts and grandparents, she was never the archetypal only child. "I had, like, 30 cousins living down the road, so I'd go and see them, always arguing and hating to share, then I'd be back home to my tidy room and unbroken toys and no fighting over my Barbie. It was like I had the best of both worlds," she said. Adele grew up into a smart, funny, chatty and confident child with a broad cockney accent, an infectiously filthy laugh and unbeatable sense of humour. "We are all really bolshie [fiery]," she said. "I have never been insecure, ever, about how I look, about what I want to do with myself. My mum told me to only ever do things for myself, not for others." Rather than slinking into the background, amidst the cacophony of all those family voices, Adele just shouted louder to get herself heard.

*"I have never been insecure, ever, about how I look, about what I want to do with myself."*

It became apparent from an early age that not only did Adele possess a big personality, she also possessed the gift of a big and soulful singing voice. Penny – being so in tune with her daughter – recognized and nurtured her talent from the start. "She was the most encouraging person," Adele says now. "She was so young when she had me…. She was always telling me to explore, and not to stick with one thing, like other mums." Not only did Penny take Adele along to music concerts from an early age, she also saved to buy her musical instruments and bought her daughter her first guitar – a little red Fisher Price model – when she was four. "My mum always had to do things whether she wanted to or not to get money to bring me up," says Adele.

Young Adele always had the radio on and loved listening to pop music. But even as a youngster her interest in music ran deeper than merely singing along. She explained, "I used to listen to how [other singers'] tones would change from angry to excited to joyful to upset." When she was five years old, 'Dreams', by Gabrielle – the 90s' singer with the iconic bejewelled eye patch – caught Adele's imagination. The chirpy schoolgirl not only asked her mum for her own eye patch and learned the words to 'Dreams', she also managed to emulate the London singer's vocal delivery and performance style. Gabrielle inspired Adele's first live performance, albeit a performance in front of her mum's friends in her toy-stuffed bedroom. "[My musical career] comes from impersonating the Spice Girls and Gabrielle. I did little concerts in my room for my mum and her friends. My mum's quite arty, she'd get all these lamps and shine them up to make one big spotlight. They'd all sit on the bed. My mum thought I was amazing."

She might be globally renowned for her big, bluesy, jazz and soul numbers now, but Adele has never been a musical snob. In 1996, along with the rest of Great Britain, she became swept up in Spice Girls mania. As an eight-year-old she adored Baby, Sporty, Posh, Ginger and Scary and took up their "Girl Power" slogan, learning the words to their songs, plastering their posters over her walls and buying all the merchandise. Being such a die-hard fan, it is no wonder Adele describes her first taste of heartbreak as being the moment Geri left the band. Never fickle, Adele carried on listening to the Girls' music until they called it a day and – proving she was no fair-weather fan – also attended the band's one-off reunion tour in 2007. "I was that generation," Adele explained. "Cheesy as it sounds, I was sitting in Tottenham, had never left the UK, but I felt I could go anywhere in the world and meet another eight-year-old and have something to talk about.

I remember noticing that music united people and I loved the feeling of that and found a massive comfort in it. A euphoric feeling, even. At eight or nine!"

Adele was always looking to refine and define her musical palate and, as a pre-teen, she also discovered American R&B, with Destiny's Child and Lauryn Hill being her particular favourites. Even though she was a little too young to understand many of the things Hill sang about, she was inspired. "*The Miseducation of Lauryn Hill* is my favourite album ever," she said. "Even though I was pretty young and oblivious to record sales and notoriety and stuff like that. That was a record I grew up listening to. I listened to it with my family. My [step]dad bought it for my mum on his way home from work one day and he bought me *Flubber*, the film. I suppose it would be more normal for a child of that age to be more interested in a VCR of a film about gel [slime] than a record but I [wasn't]. I nicked the record and I analyzed it for about a month, when I was eight, and wondered when I would ever make a record about something I was that passionate about, even though I had no idea that I was going to make a record when I was older."

Adele, Penny and Penny's new partner (who Adele now refers to as "dad") moved house many times, meaning Adele changed schools a lot, too. Not that she minded. In an interview with *Rolling Stone* magazine, she said, "I loved moving. I think that's why I can't stay in one place now. I don't think of my childhood like, 'Oh, I went to 10 different schools.' My mum always made it fun." And Adele has never taken the sacrifices her mum made for granted. "She fell pregnant with me when she would have been applying for uni, but chose to have me instead. She never, ever reminds me of that. I try to remember it." At nine, Penny – who had always had a bohemian streak – moved house and took Adele to the funky coastal city of Brighton, where they lived for two years. However, despite having a beach minutes from her doorstep and being surrounded by nice houses, cool shops and cafés, Adele missed her working-class, multicultural Tottenham neighbourhood, the sights and sounds, colours, flavours, and influences of her old haunts. She was shocked at how few black and Asian faces she saw in Brighton and

yearned to go back. Two years later, Penny and Adele moved back to London, this time moving south and setting up home in Brixton for a while before moving to nearby South Norwood, where they rented a flat above a convenience store. Adele felt at home again. "In Tottenham and South London I was the only white girl in my school. It was always like that but it didn't feel strange at all. They were rough neighbourhoods if you don't live there, but when you live there not at all."

Adele enrolled at Chestnut Grove school in Balham, and while the stars might have decreed that one day she would set the world alight, it was not going to be due to her academic achievements. While she was undeniably bright and streetwise, she didn't excel in any one subject and her grades never really rose above average. She was more interested in getting home, sticking on a CD and singing along to her favourite pop stars. At 14, Adele *attempted* to fall in love with the American metal music her mates adored. She declared herself a Slipknot fan, and decked herself out in the scene's uniform of dark baggy clothes. Secretly, and she wouldn't admit this for a couple of years, she preferred listening to Celine Dion. Like most teens, she headed into town on weekends and passed many an hour perusing the shelves at HMV music store. It was there that she had a musical epiphany. She explains, "I was a grunger back then and I pretended I loved Slipknot and Korn, but really they terrified me. I loved the fashion mostly, the dog collars and the baggy jeans and jumpers. It was what we were all doing. But then I was in HMV in the jazz section and I was like, 'Actually guys I don't like Slipknot.' I saw Etta James and Ella Fitzgerald, two-for-a-fiver in a bargain bin. It was their hair I liked at first, crimped '40s jazz hair ..."

Adele's brush with the bargain bin that Saturday afternoon was to be significant. "I never got the haircut but Etta James has become my favourite artist. It was the passion in their voices that got me. Etta James, I believe every word she sings. I was blown away. She's so sincere, so much conviction in her voice. I taught myself how to sing by listening to her. I went from being generic to thinking about lyrics rather than just singing them." James's and Fitzgerald's voices showed Adele there was more to soul singing than the elaborate vocal gymnastics displayed by the likes of Mariah Carey (whom Adele also loved). "So many people sing like that now, and I could do it if I wanted to, but the first time you hear it you're like, 'Wow!' and by the fifth time, it's like… 'get something new.' It's more impressive, somehow, if you don't try to impress. Be natural with it. Say it straight." Etta James had a visceral impact on her. "It was like she went in my chest and beat my heart up."

As a kid, Adele was always singing her favourite records into a hairbrush and belting out songs in the shower and in the car. But at 14, she got a taste of a real recording studio – and she never looked back. She was tentatively in touch with her dad, after a three-year absence from her life, and he introduced her to one of his friends – a dance music producer. The friend invited Adele over to his studio to perform a cover of Blondie's 'Heart of Glass'. After she'd laid down her vocals, her dad's mate simply described her demo as "wicked." Nothing came of the track but it did spur Adele on to take up the guitar, the bass, piano and clarinet – although she soon gave up the latter after discovering a fondness for nicotine. "I started smoking so don't really have the lungs to play clarinet," she says. Singing was no problem. "As soon as I got a microphone in my hand, I realized I wanted to do this. Most people don't like the way their voice sounds when it's recorded. I was just so excited that I wasn't bothered what it sounded like."

*"As soon as I got a microphone in my hand I realized I wanted to do this."*

Around this time Adele was also taking her first tentative steps into the realm of songwriting, admitting now, that while she was growing up – and to this day still – she finds it easier to express her feelings by writing them down. "I don't know if it's because I'm an only child but I was never, ever good at saying how I felt about things. From the age of about five, if I was told off for not sharing or I didn't tidy my room, or I spoke back to my mum, I'd always write a note as an apology."

The seeds of a future in music had been planted, and they were

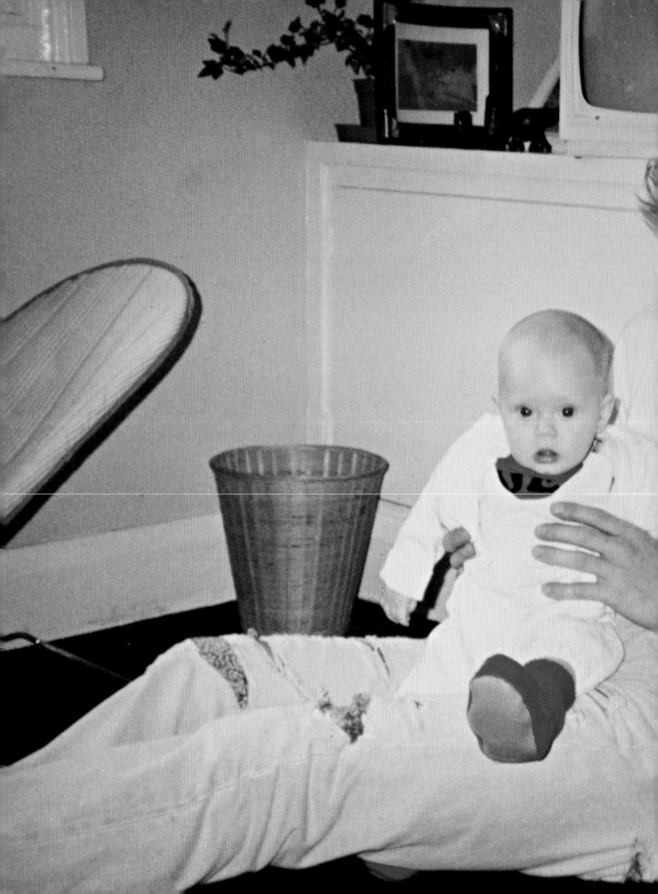

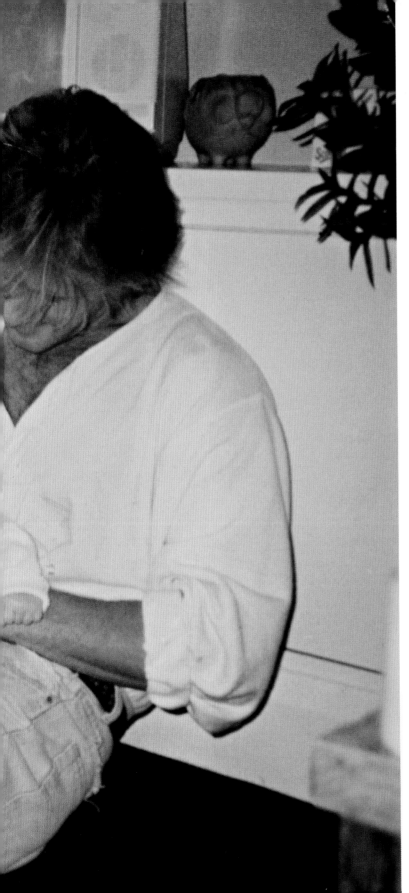

◄ Adele as a baby with her dad, Mark. Her folks may not have been musical but they had a second-to-none record collection which had a lasting impact on her.

constantly being watered. In 2002, a new reality TV show called *Pop Idol* was to have a big impact on Adele. As we all know now it was a show that took ordinary kids who wanted to sing for a living, and providing they had the talent, turned them into stars. Back then it was a new phenomenon and Adele was hooked. "Will Young was my first proper love. I was obsessed. [At school] the Gareth Gates fans were horrible to me and I wasn't having any of it. We had a fight and I was called into the head teacher's office and sent home. It was serious." At the opposite end of the musical spectrum, Adele was also infatuated with Mike Skinner of the Streets and played his famed debut album, *Original Pirate Material*, on repeat. She loved that he took normal, everyday situations and turned them into fresh, dramatic and captivating songs. And while his particular brand of urban poetry was never a genre she sought to emulate in her own music, she was inspired by the Streets to sing in her own cockney brogue, rather than trying to emulate an American accent. "I was so in love with Mike Skinner that I wrote him a letter," Adele admitted. "When I told my friend about it she cussed me, so I went and pretended to do the washing up and cried."

While Adele was always encouraged to express her musical and creative side at home, it was never the case at school. She has described her teachers as "a bit rubbish" saying, "They gave me a really hard time, trying to bribe me, saying that if I wanted to sing I had to play clarinet to sing in the choir. So I left." That isn't quite the full story, of course. Adele didn't just *leave* school, she left school and joined a prestigious performing arts school, which recognized her staggering potential and nurtured her talents rather than dismissed them.

"I remember wanting to go to the Sylvia Young Theatre School because Baby Spice went there, but my mum couldn't afford it," she said. So she did a bit of research and discovered a place called the BRIT School in Croydon, South London. You didn't need money to get in, but you did need talent and confidence in bundles. And so emerged plan B. After managing to land herself an audition and blowing away the interview panel with her voice, she was invited to join the ranks of its fledgling stars. At the tender age of 14, Adele's life was about to change forever.

◄ After her parents separated when she was a toddler, Adele maintained a relationship with her father. It was only to last until she was eleven.

# 3

# BRIT School and Beyond

In September 2002, Adele walked through the doors of the famous BRIT School for the first time feeling like she was stepping onto the set of *Fame*. "There were kids doing pirouettes in the f\*\*king hallway and doing mime and having sing-offs in the foyer," she recalls. At 5' 9", a size 14, and with no formal dance training to her name, Adele was never going to be one of the ballet girls, but that didn't mean the streetwise teen didn't secretly – just a little bit – absolutely love her new environment. She had finally found a place where she belonged, an educational institution that clearly encouraged kids to follow their passions. It wasn't all legwarmers and high-kicks, anyway. Unlike NYC's fictional Fame School of Performing Arts, the BRIT School, in the slightly less-glam-than-Manhattan locale of Selwood in Croydon, South London, is a vocational school, and its aim is to set students off on bona fide careers in entertainment, arts and communications. Which means that even though its timetable might include exotic-sounding lessons such as music management and recording, pupils still have to study hard for their exams.

Funded by the state and supported by the British Record Industry Trust, the BRIT School coaches 14- to 19-year-olds in everything from media and visual arts to musical theatre. It opened its doors in 1991 and its glittering roll call of former students reads like a Who's Who of modern-day pop greats.

▶ Adele channeling her inner photo-booth-loving teen – and showing just why she was right to land a place at the BRIT School – in a somewhat tattered post-graduation publicity shot.

Its most famous pre-Adele graduate was fellow North London soulstress, Amy Winehouse. The internationally renowned Leona Lewis and Jessie J, 2011 Mercury Prize nominee Katy B, Kate Nash, Shingai Shoniwa of the Noisettes, Imogen Heap and chart-smashing Brighton rap duo Rizzle Kicks have passed through its corridors too. Commentators have estimated that between them, these artists have sold more than 10 million albums in the UK alone.

Back in the early 2000s, before even the most celebrated astrologer could have predicted what lay ahead of them, Adele became good pals with classmate Jessie J – back then plain old Jessica Ellen Cornish. They weren't on the same course as each other but the two girls clicked. Kindred spirits, neither of them were naturally academic but they both loved to sing and write, meeting up in empty classrooms to jam. Thinking back to her early impressions of Adele, Jessie said, "That's why we got on because singing was our outlet. I'm not great at science and maths and everything else, and I had two older sisters that were very academic and were both head girls – and that was my rebellion. It was like, 'I want to do music, and I want to do something that they didn't do.' And I think me and Adele found that bond for jamming and music in the music room."

Jessie, like most of the kids at the BRIT school, loved Adele's larger-than-life personality. As you'd expect from a girl who'd never had any problems with shyness, Adele made her mark on the place as soon as she walked through the doors. She was boisterous, fun, funny, and popular with girls and boys, and she never lacked a boyfriend. Remembering schoolgirl Adele, Jessie said, "She was cool. She was kind of loud and everyone knew her. She was the girl everyone loved and was up for a laugh and you could hear her laugh from a mile down the corridor."

Adele and Shingai, future front-woman of the Noisettes, were also good pals. In fact Shingai had an even greater influence on Adele than Jessie – she was responsible for making the talented teen realize she could hone her voice into something special and turn her love of writing her feelings down, into affecting songs. "Just hearing Shingai and her music really made me want

◀ Fellow BRIT alumnus and north London girl, the late Amy Winehouse. The singer was a huge influence on Adele.

to be a writer and not just sing Destiny's Child songs," Adele recalled. It was no big surprise that the talented pair were so close – they lived right next door to one another above the Co-op shop in South Norwood and would regularly go round to each other's flats. "That place should have two blue plaques," Shingai has said. "Awesome days: she had a piano, I had a drum kit. We always used to jam."

Adele was living and breathing music, and training pretty much 24/7 – even if it did just feel like having fun. Unsurprisingly, her voice became bigger and better. While the walls of the BRIT School rang to the sounds of hundreds of sweetly trilling voices, none stopped people in their tracks quite like Adele's. Heartbreakingly husky, soulful and soaring, it was a sound teachers and pupils alike came to know and love. In an interview with *Rolling Stone* magazine, former classmate Ben Thomas, now Adele's guitarist, recalled, "There were some people at school who really pushed hard. You could tell they really wanted it. Adele never really had that. But she was a great performer and everyone would be completely silent and in awe when she performed."

One of the reasons Adele didn't push as hard as some was because, while she adored singing, she didn't really believe you could do it for a living. She reckoned she was more likely to go into a behind-the-scenes role, music production or A&R. She recalled, "I knew I'd pass all the music and performance stuff. And because of that I thought I'd get work somewhere in the music industry. Getting signed was never an ambition."

As such, her time at school wasn't without its ups and downs. She was still required to study mathematics and English and all the usual curriculum subjects. Unfortunately, she was no more academic at her new school than she had been at Chestnut Grove. It resulted in an attitude so laid-back it verged on tardiness. She would sometimes skip lessons to spend her mornings lying in bed, turning up to school when she felt like it. However, after coming perilously close to being booted out, she began to take school seriously. The turning point came when she arrived late to a school concert in which she was set to perform and almost missed her singing slot. Faced with the wrath of her angry teachers,

▶ This 2007 publicity shot seems to capture Adele's BRIT School spirit perfectly: feisty, a little stubborn, and with one eye on making it big.

Adele was forced to rethink her attitude. She remembers, "My heart exploded. It was pretty horrible. I almost did get kicked out of school for that. Now I'm always on time."

Adele didn't take to what she called "dissecting songs" in class, either. "I didn't pay attention in class because I don't believe in learning about music through some old man's criteria. I think that's bulls**t," she says. "I went to use free equipment and meet amazing people. I went there for the free recording studios, free rehearsal rooms. To learn about songwriting, I listen to songwriters." Neither did she believe in singing lessons – she only ever took part in one and made a pact never to take another. "It made me think about my voice too much. You can teach *yourself*," she said. "I listen to Etta James to get a bit of soul, Ella Fitzgerald for my chromatic scales, Roberta Flack for control."

Happily, when she was 16 going on 17, one particular recording lesson captured the often-stubborn schoolgirl's imagination. The class was required to write, perform and record a track – a challenge she relished. Her songwriting getting stronger all the time and her imagination usually buzzing, all it took was a conversation with Penny to result in a hit-in-waiting. To set the scene, Adele had toyed with the idea of moving to Liverpool to do a musical degree after leaving college – but had subsequently gone off the idea. Penny, who left home when she was 18, however, thought it would be a good move for Adele to move out and stand on her own two feet, as she had done. Their subsequent tête-à-tête gave Adele the seed of an idea. She was a London girl through and through, she told her mum. She could never leave her hometown.

She wrote 'Hometown Glory' in ten minutes flat on her guitar. It was both a protest song and a soulful hymn to London, and all its glamour and grizzle. She sang a line about its people being at odds with their government, a reference to the protests against the Iraq War that had had a big impact on her at the time. It was a haunting, melancholy track and was to feature on her debut album three years down the line. When she finally got round to performing it at school, Adele's classmates and teachers were left spellbound. They'd heard that spine-tingling voice before, but

**Previous page (left):** During the BRIT School years: Adele chilling in a cool rooftop hangout, coffee and cigarette close at hand, 2006.

**Previous page (right):** Adele looking moody and cool in an early publicity shot.

▶ Adele showing her more sensitive side in a 2007 studio shot.

never married with such a powerful and personal song. One of her classmates, Allan Rose, told the *Sun* newspaper, "It was clear she was going to be a star. Some people were that step above everyone else and Adele was one of them." Suddenly no one was in any doubt that they had a huge star on their hands – her teachers knew that if she applied herself Adele could be world-class. Encouraged, she penned two more tracks while in her final year at the BRIT School – 'My Same' and 'Daydreamer'. It took a friend of hers to get the ball rolling on her career, however. Adele called her pal "My Mr MySpace." He set her up with her first MySpace page, uploaded her three demos and sent the tracks on to an Internet magazine, *Platforms*, which became the first site to host Adele's work. Putting her music out on to the Web – a "place" combed by A&Rs and music moguls listening out for the next new thing – was all it took. From there, things began to snowball. Adele's music career was in motion, even if she didn't realize it at the time. Sure she was becoming more confident in her singing ability, but she was still 99 percent skeptical that an ordinary girl like her could make a living from singing – and even more cynical that she could use social networking to further her way to the top.

Once her songs were in the public domain, however, she had no choice but to face up to a simple fact: she had a rare talent and the world wanted to hear it. The buzz around Adele grew and grew over the next year – until it became deafening. She was still at school, not doing any gigs and not really putting herself out there on the circuit, and yet she and Mr MySpace were being bombarded by emails from record companies. "My mate was like, 'I've got all these people from record companies emailing me, what should I say?'" she says. "I thought, 'Yeah, whatever.' I didn't believe you could get signed through MySpace."

She was to have her expectations turned upside down. During her final year at the BRIT School, she was approached by the then head of A&R at XL Recordings, Nick Hugget. XL is a successful independent label, with a super-cool roster that back then boasted the likes of the White Stripes, Dizzee Rascal, the Prodigy, and two of Adele's favourite artists at the time,

Jack Penate and Jamie T. Adele had never heard of XL, though – the only record label she was familiar with back then was Richard Branson's Virgin Records. And so when she received a string of emails from the label asking her to go in for a chat, she initially ignored them, thinking it was all a big wind-up. She said, "I thought it was some dirty Internet pervert. I saw there were e-mails from Island and XL, but I'd never heard of them so I didn't call them back." But XL persisted, knowing they had stumbled upon a diamond. The emails continued to pour in and eventually, Adele gave in and agreed to go along to their offices. However she took her BRIT pal and future-guitarist Ben along with her for moral support, admitting, "I never, ever thought I'd get signed. The A&R guy emailed and I was ignoring it. I didn't realize they did all these amazing names."

*"I never, ever thought I'd get signed. The A&R guy emailed and I was ignoring it."*

For Adele, just 18 and fresh out of college, the whole thing was a nerve-wracking experience. It was only once she got to the offices and looked at the discs and posters of XL's world-famous artists mounted on the walls, that she realized this was the real deal. She was teetering on the cusp of something big. It was June 2006 and the initial chats went well. At the next meeting, XL introduced Adele to management maestro Jonathan Dickins. Dickins, who has a history marinated in music (his grandfather co-founded the magazine *New Musical Express*) and Adele clicked, immediately falling into a conversation about their musical idols. Like everyone else who meets her, Dickins was blown away by the warmth of Adele's personality and her backbone – her determination that if she was going to do this, she would do it her way. He also fell in love with her sense of humour, her infectious laugh, and of course, her incomparable singing voice.

Recalling their initial meeting, he said, "Nick said I should check this girl out. I just got a MySpace URL. We had one meeting and just got on great. She was a massive fan of Jamie T. She was 18, just out of college, and wanted to make a career in music. We discussed music in that first meeting. I always listen to artists. The other key factor for me regarding management is listening to what an artist wants – I've got better at that. Adele is incredible… It's unbelievable how focused she is in terms of what she thinks is right for her career. So, I listened and threw in some ideas, and generally it just clicked."

XL and Dickins arranged a showcase so they could hear Adele's voice in a live arena. Once she stepped onto the stage at the venue in Brixton and sang her first note, they were blown away. "She's just brilliant," Dickins would later say of Adele, "I don't think there's any science to it. She is probably the best singer, or one of the best singers I've ever heard in my life. That voice is incredible."

For XL there was no denying her potential either. They were looking for an artist with originality and longevity and in Adele they knew they'd found both. A few months after their initial meeting, Adele signed on the dotted line: September 2006 and she'd done it, she'd landed a recording contract. Signing Adele was a no-brainer for XL co-founder and CEO, Richard Russell. "There's something about her voice. It connected to you very directly. Her subject matter – being hurt – she talks about it in a way that's so easy to relate to," he said in an interview with the *Independent*. "It's very honest. She's incredibly focused. She's got very strong ideas about what she wants to do and strong ideas about what she wants the result to be." The skeptical London girl was having to adjust her impression of the music business at an astronomical rate. The three months since she'd left college had passed by in head-exploding blur, barely allowing her a moment to stop to reflect on her time at the BRIT School. She might have moaned about some of the lessons, giggled at some of the prima donnas leaping about the canteen, but nowadays when she pauses for a moment, she has nothing but good things to say about her old school. "While at first I was very like, 'I ain't goin'

**Previous pages:** Adele with her trusty guitar in 2006. During her BRIT school years, she played whenever and *wherever* she could.

◄ The green-eyed soul girl in 2007: Adele's teachers and fellow students at school all knew she had a stellar career ahead if she applied herself.

'ere! It's a stage school! I can do it on my own!' I think I do owe it completely to the BRIT School for making me who I am today, as cheesy and embarrassing at it may sound," she told *Blues and Soul* magazine. "Because, while my mum is the most supportive mum on earth, she wouldn't have known how to channel me. With her I'd probably have gone down the classical music route, or maybe Disney, or musical theatre. But at the BRIT School I found my direction, because the music course was really wicked … It's not your typical stage school full of kids that are pushed into it by their parents. It's a school full of kids that will dance at a freezing-cold town hall barefoot for eight hours solid. And, whereas before I was going to a school with bums and kids that were rude and wanted to grow up and mug people, it was really inspiring to wake up every day to go to school with kids that actually wanted to be productive at something and wanted to be somebody."

The BRIT School was a proven breeding ground for A-List talent, but this one-time cynical teen was suddenly leading the

▲ Adele always found it easier to express her true feelings by getting them down on paper. This photograph is from 2006.

▶ Early on in her career, Adele decided she wouldn't conform to a popstar stereotype, instead letting her music, not her image, do the talking. A publicity shot from 2007.

new pack – and there hadn't been any of the typical low points along the way. None of the long, self-esteem-crippling bouts of unemployment or what-the-hell-next periods that most grads face; Adele never had to wait tables or sign on. "It literally all fell in to my lap," she says now. "I was always singing, I always knew I would be involved in music but I thought I'd be a receptionist, or work in a shop or something, and then on my off days go and play a little acoustic show for my family and friends. I didn't even bother to dream about being a singer because everyone I know has dreams and none of theirs has come true, so why the hell would mine?"

Adele didn't immediately explode onto the scene in a blaze of jaw-dropping, number one-bagging glory, however. Quite the opposite. After signing with XL, she fell into a creative lull and became besieged by the dreaded writer's block – she didn't pen another song until May of the following year. She kept her toe in the water by playing a few local gigs – audiences loved her onstage banter nearly as much as her foundation-shaking voice – but for the rest of the time, she watched *Sex and the City*, hung out with her friends, smoked cigarettes, and drank red wine. Oh, and she fell in love – with a boy who charmed her, and then cheated on her, breaking her heart in the process. It was May 2007 and all of a sudden she had her cure for writer's block– even if it was a bitter pill to swallow. Soon after her nineteenth birthday party, she sat down, with her heart battered and bruised, and penned seven tracks in three weeks. She might have been in the doldrums but she had an almost complete first album, and a brainwave for the album title.

Adele's mood was blue in early summer 2007, but her career was suddenly a blaze of Technicolor, although it had been touch and go. She admitted, "I was almost ready to give up, because I just couldn't write any songs, and then I got into a relationship and it was horrible. By June, I had 12 songs."

Once she had those songs, everything else began to fall into place. She was suddenly being introduced left, right and centre to the best producers and songwriters in the biz – people she had idolized for years. There was no time like it to get in the studio. There, she hooked up with Mark Ronson, the cool musician and producer who had produced one of her favourite hip-hop albums in the form of 2003 disc, *Here Comes the Fuzz*. She was also introduced to famed songwriter Francis "Eg" White – the man behind her beloved Will Young's killer hit, 'Leave Right Now'. Eg was to help turn her raw, heartfelt lyrics into grand, sparkling productions.

Suddenly, Adele was in demand and things were looking up. Even she began to believe she could do this. And then came a "pinch-me" moment. She received a call from the producers of noted music television show *Later with Jools Holland*, inviting her – despite the fact she hadn't released a single record – to make her live singing debut on the show. The producers took a chance on her based on the strength of her demo CD. It was June 8, 2007, and Adele couldn't believe what was happening. Not only had it been one of her favourite shows while she was growing up, not only did she love Jools himself, but she had been told she'd be positioned on stage between Paul McCartney and Björk. The loveable motor mouth was rendered momentarily speechless.

*"For some reason they put me at the end, right in front of the audience, with Björk on my left, Paul McCartney on my right and my mum crying in front of me. I met them afterwards and couldn't stop crying."*

She performed an acoustic version of 'Daydreamer', and, keeping it real, she wore her favourite uniform of leggings, long top and comfy shoes. While she later admitted she had been almost sick with nerves in her dressing room, you would never have guessed. Her moment in the spotlight betrayed none of this. Instead she put in a performance of gentle, understated majesty, and left the TV audience breathless. As she strummed the final note on her guitar, they burst into whistles and applause.

It was an emotional experience. Talking to the *Guardian* about her *Later* experience, Adele said, "They usually put you in the middle of the room, but for some reason they put me at the end, right in front of the audience, with Björk on my left, Paul McCartney on my right and my mum crying in front of me. I met them afterwards, and couldn't stop crying." It wasn't just Adele who was emotional after the event, the *Later* crew were choked. Their gamble had paid off. After the show, producer Alison Howe said, "I would hope that by this time next year, she will have sold as many records as Amy [Winehouse], and I don't see why she shouldn't. When we fall for somebody, we have to have them. She's a classic. She doesn't fit anywhere, she just has a great voice."

Like bees to honey, the offers of TV shows and support-slots began to swarm in Adele's direction. In November 2007, she thought she had died and gone to heaven when she was invited to support her pop idol Will Young at a charity gig at London's Union Chapel. She jumped at the chance of course, and her performance was a success. Her ballads and between-song banter went down brilliantly with the crowd, she got to hang out with Will, and on top of that she also met super-producer Jim Abbiss – who famously produced Arctic Monkeys' Mercury-winning debut album *Whatever People Say I Am, That's What I'm Not* – who has been one of her go-to producers ever since. She was also invited to perform on popular entertainment show *Friday Night with Jonathan Ross*.

And then came some more thrilling news. On December 10, 2007, despite only having put debut single 'Hometown Glory' out on limited release in October, she was told she was the winner of the inaugural BRITs Critics' Choice Award, an award which industry insiders and musical tastemakers were to bestow on the artist or band they believed to the be the hottest property of the year. Adele was flabbergasted. She had a ticket to the 2008 BRIT awards – not as a guest or a school kid in the front row, but as a winner. It was a great early Christmas present.

There was another wake-me-up-I-must-be-dreaming moment at the end of the year: the announcement that she was the top artist on the prestigious BBC Sound of 2008 list, ahead of artists such as Duffy and Foals. In the accompanying BBC interview, she was refreshingly open about her inspirations, her hopes for the future and her behaviour in relationships. When asked what inspired her music, she replied, "Love, I like love. I like drama. I like causing drama as well. It's always about love or hate, really, and if I'm not in either I have to create it. Not bad drama – just every other drama that everyone else has. Rubbish boyfriends and stopping talking to your mates and stuff. But I create a lot of it as well, and I exaggerate a lot of it sometimes and annoy them so they're even meaner to me. I do it on purpose sometimes."

*"I hope it's always about the music and I hope I don't become scandalous and it takes me like an hour to get out my front door."*

On the pressure of being named the first BRIT's Critics Choice Awards winner, she was laid-back. "I'm not really feeling very pressurized, I thought I would. I'm really excited, I hope it's always about the music and I hope I don't become scandalous and it takes me like an hour to get out my front door. I hope I always enjoy it, and I think I will. I'm having a laugh." She wanted her music to connect but she didn't want to see her face in the paper every day. "I love *Heat* magazine. I love these magazines because they look rubbish, some of these people who you think are untouchable. So you feel really good when you look at them, and I like seeing what they get up to when they ain't working," she said. "I just don't want that to ever happen to me. If it ever got to the point where I couldn't do anything, I'd quit. Music's wicked and I love doing it and I have a laugh, but my life's more important to me than my music. So I'd leave until everyone had forgotten about me."

It didn't look like there was much chance of that, not now that she had a collection of soul-stirring songs to her name. On January 28, 2008, she shared them with the world. The album was simply but unforgettably called *19*.

# 4

# The Breakthrough: *19*

The album *19* opens with the gentle, lovelorn strum of 'Daydreamer' – one of the songs Adele wrote at school. Over an acoustic guitar she paints the picture of a dreamy, young guy, "a jaw-dropper", who would be elusive but worth catching and could do anything he put his mind to. Oh, and he was a gallant gentleman too! It was clear Adele was in lust with the subject of her song but the subtly ambiguous lilt in her voice also told you she knew not to pin her hopes on him. This one sounded too good to be true – and we all know how that has a tendency to turn out. As it happens, the track was about a bisexual guy she'd had a fling with during her BRIT School years. They had told each other they'd fallen for one another but a few hours afterwards her boy had run off with one of her gay friends. "I was like, 'We're not even going out yet and you've cheated on me already!' So 'Daydreamer' is about everything I wanted him to be. The daydream of him," she remembers. The next track, 'Best for Last', saw her grappling with more mature, complex emotions. It was one of the seven songs she wrote in quick succession after finding out her ex had been cheating on her. On first listen this sounds like Adele giving her philandering lover a piece of her mind. Even the opening guitar line is arch. She pledges her love for him and invites him to do the same, while knowing it just isn't going to happen. You can almost sense her raised eyebrow

▶ In a publicity shoot during the *19* album campaign in 2008, Adele refines her urban chic look.

▲ Adele during a live session at
Indig0₂ in London, November 2008.

while she's singing. Whatever the cad's cheesy lines or excuses, by the chorus, we know it's not going to fly with our feisty heroine. Over a jazzy, funky background, she tells it like it is, explaining to her hapless ex that he was only ever filling in while she waited for someone more significant to come along. It may not be true, but it's powerful.

But it's not a black-and-white track. Reflecting the conflicting emotions of a breakup, there's another change in mood in verse two as she admits her feelings for him are more profound than she has let on. By the third chorus and middle eight Adele admits the truth about her feelings. In spite of herself, she wants her man back. Love hurts and she is suffering. The next track, 'Chasing Pavements', was the official first single release, with a big sunburst of a chorus. As for the curious and cryptic lyrics that form the main refrain of the chorus – it was about the same guy, and there is a typical Adele-ism behind the lyrics. She explained, "It's about

▲ Adele at Washington, D.C.'s 9:30 Club in January of 2009.

◄ With her idol Will Young at the 2008 BRIT Awards after Will presented her with the inaugural BRITs Critics' Choice Award.

the boy who cheated on me. I found out and I went to a club and punched him and I got thrown out." She ended up racing down Oxford Street, chasing nobody, she realized, but the pavement. Hey presto, a catchy song title was born.

She worked on the track with super songsmith Eg White – and you can tell the pair meant business. With the plaintive poignant verses and almost Burt Bacharach-esque sweeping chorus, full of strings and instrumentation, it sounded like nothing else out there.

While her fellow chart newcomer, Duffy, had a very stylized retro-pop 60s' sound, Amy MacDonald was doing Celtic-flavoured folk, and the rest of the Top 40 was made up of US R&B, hip-hop, and the remnants of the indie music scene, Adele's style was hard to define, rousing in an almost old-fashioned way. "I wanted to work with Eg White when I heard what stuff he'd done, because I wanted that radio song," she recalled. "I wanted that big kind of commercial tune to get me noticed by people. Because, while personally I'd happily still sing to ten people in a pub like I used to, I do want as many people as possible to hear my music. Not so they'd buy my album, but because I do want to be known as a musician. So in that way 'Chasing Pavements' was quite intentional." She remembers going along to Eg's studio with a couple of chords and a chorus. "He took those two chords and a chorus and made it into 'Chasing Pavements'."

▲ Adele unleashing that inimitable laugh with host Reggie Yates at the 2008 BRIT Awards nominations.

▲ Adele in London, January 14, 2008.

▶ Adele enjoying a glass of bubbly backstage at the BRIT Awards 2008.

◄ Adele at the 2009 Nationwide Mercury Prize with her trophy for being nominated for *19*. Rapper Speech Debelle went on to win.

▲ Finding her fashion feet. The big, cozy coat has been swapped for a glam fur-trimmed number in 2008.

A combination of factors – loads of radio play, miles of newspaper write-ups, and a high-profile outing on the *Friday Night with Jonathan Ross* show – meant 'Chasing Pavements' was the chart-stormer Adele had hoped for. It landed at No. 2 after being released on January 11, 2008, and its quirky video, which sees the chanteuse singing at the scene of a car accident – all wavy hair, smoky eye makeup and comfy shoes – caught the attention of hip-hop royalty and musical tastemaker, Kanye West, who featured it on his blog, along with the statement, "This s**t is dope!!!!!!" It was quite the seal of approval and her YouTube hits skyrocketed.

The next track up is the sultry 'Cold Shoulder', produced by hotshot Mark Ronson and featuring trip-hoppy beats and searing strings that recall Massive Attack's 'Unfinished Symphony'. Lyrically it was about *him* again – and his duplicitous ways, as Adele demands he tells her the sordid truth about his cheating. You can imagine the scene playing out in a domestic setting, Adele hand on hip, eyes full of fury, her man standing there, wretchedly. The chorus is full of strained drama and you can hear the anger in her voice, her cockney accent slipping subtly into the delivery.

When the track was released as the second single on April 21, 2008, Ronson was the man of the moment, having been feted for his work on Amy Winehouse's *Back to Black* – but Adele was adamant she didn't just work with him because it was the cool thing to do. "The fact is, I met him the same day his *Version* album came out in the UK, at a time when no one was expecting it to do that well and not even Amy's record was that big [then]. It was purely because I think he's amazingly talented and he's got a real ear," she told *Blues and Soul*. "And personally I just think he's got nicer with his success and completely deserves all the acclaim he gets. Particularly when, to me, in *Back to Black* he's produced one of the greatest albums of all time."

The admiration went two ways. Recalling the moment he met Adele for the first time, Ronson says, "She was 18, chain-smoking Marlboro Lights and watching *Jerry Springer*. She said, 'This is the song I want you to produce.' I was struck by her determination. With all the manufactured, computer-adulterated pop out there, it's great that when a person comes along with

▶ Adele at a January 2008 photo shoot.

an incredible voice and real songs it still trumps everything. It's great for the music industry that it happened. And I love Adele as a friend, I think she's f**king amazing." As far as Ronson was concerned, Adele was destined for greatness no matter who she hooked up with in the studio. "I championed her early on but she didn't need me for her success," he said. "It was always going to happen. Sometimes the stars just line up and that's it."

The next track, 'Crazy For You', is another acoustic number and a simple, heart-on-the-sleeve love song. It's followed by the lump-in-the-throat-making ballad 'Melt My Heart to Stone', Adele's favourite track on the album. It's about the excuses you make for someone you're in love with, but who treats you badly – and that pivotal moment when you realize your relationship is a one-way street. Even though the relationship had been over a long time by the time *19* came out, Adele still found the track painful to listen to and sing. She explained, "Now I have to talk about the boy that I hate all the time. I mean we're friends but I do still hate him a little bit. 'Melt My Heart to Stone' is my favourite – it's really hard to sing, and makes me cry loads."

'First Love' followed, and was a snapshot of Adele at an earlier period of the relationship, when it was she who had the cold feet.

'Right As Rain' is jaunty pop with a twist, illustrating Adele's self-confessed drama-queen streak.

The next track was one of the last songs Adele recorded for the album, a cover of Bob Dylan's 'Make You Feel My Love'. It doesn't really sound like anything else on the album. Swollen with emotion, it's stripped back with just a simple piano line, and almost hymnal in pace. It certainly brought the album to a calm, reflective close. She was never in any doubt the track would have a place on there either, not once her manager Jonathan had introduced her to the song and it had left her speechless. She said, "I love other people's songs but I don't like covering other people's songs. But I heard that and then I read the lyrics and they're the most beautiful lyrics I've ever read or heard." It was to become one of Adele's most-played songs and its understated intensity paved the way for more mature work to come. Released in November 2008, it initially reached No. 26 in the UK. However, after various contestants covered it during the 2008 UK version of the *X Factor* – and in TV talent shows across the globe – it saw a massive increase in popularity and returned to the charts where it peaked at No. 4. The simple video sees Adele singing the song, live, in an anonymous New York hotel room, overlooking the bright lights and buzz of the city.

The finger-clicking 'My Same' came next, another of the tracks Adele recorded at the BRIT School. Jazzy and bluesy, she admits it sounds like a love song, but in actual fact is about her best female friend. She revealed, "It's about me and my friend Laura – it's an homage to Ella Fitzgerald and Louis Armstrong. You wouldn't think we get on, we're complete opposites, but we do." The penultimate track on the album, 'Tired', is Adele's final kiss-off to her wayward lover. Her proud cockney accent contrasts coolly with the song's elegant swirling strings – almost a sonic metaphor for Adele herself.

The album opened with a track she wrote as a schoolgirl, and so it closed with one: the iconic, piano-led 'Hometown Glory' – an ode to London and its people. The track was to be released twice, once as a limited edition release in October 2007 on Jamie T's Pacemaker record label and once again in July 2008. The track

◀ With designer Barbara Tfank in early 2009. The designer created Adele's 2009 Grammy Awards dress after being introduced to her by US *Vogue* editor, Anna Wintour.

◀ In the glow of the stage lights at a concert in Texas in March 2009, Adele indulges her audience with some of her trademark banter.

peaked at No. 19 in the UK but brought Adele global recognition after it was used on the soundtrack to the hugely popular TV show *Grey's Anatomy* and on the UK show *Skins*. The song is now synonymous with Adele herself: classic, cool, chic, and cockney through and through.

The album was a heady cocktail of teen hormones, heartache and love for her hometown – and *19* was the perfect name for it. "I couldn't come up with anything else," Adele joked around its release date. But she was just being self-deprecating; secretly she had strived to come up with a name as simple and iconic as Björk's *Debut* and Lauryn Hill's *The Miseducation of Lauryn Hill*. "They're ones that everyone just knows that don't make you think too much, and are just quite obvious," she said. "And to me this album does very much represent my age. I was only 19 years old when I was writing it, and I just kinda remember becoming a bit of a woman during that time."

Recording was a cathartic experience. "For me it was just about making a record of songs to get a boy off my chest and include all the different kinds of music that I love." She was sanguine about the unnamed subject of her album, saying, "I got an album out of him. I used him more than he used me." However, she did admit her heartfelt lyrics were usually the result of a terrible fight or grim revelation, after which she would lock herself away. "I will sit in my room on my own for ages, because otherwise I am rude to people. I can't be around anyone, I have to be on my own. And I'll write. That's how that atmosphere gets created. Something has to completely take over my life for me to write about it," she said. Who needs relationship counselling when you had a talent like Adele's? But while writing the album was a form of therapy – without the couch and doctor's bills – even Adele didn't realize how hurt she had been until she listened back to the songs. "I don't like confrontation 'cause it always ends in fights so I never say how I feel and songs are the way I tell people how I feel. That's how I get things out 'cause in reality I can't really admit things to myself. Makes things seem better in a song. I didn't realize it was a sour relationship I was in until I listened to the songs."

With 'Chasing Pavements' dominating the airwaves in early 2008 and promising great things for the album, Adele seemed like the complete package. But even then, right at the beginning of her career when she potentially had more to lose, she was super honest. Rather than shout her mouth off about how "inspired" she was, how "special" the songs were, or generally carp on about just how all-round "amazing" she was (as some lesser singers are wont to do), Adele told anyone who would listen that she still considered herself a work-in-progress. "I had no specific plans for my album. In fact, I still don't know exactly what kind of artist I wanted to be," she said. "So there's pop, there's a bit of electro, there's jazz, there's folk, and of course there's soul. But, at the same time, while there are those obvious elements of soul in my music and certainly in my voice, I never at any stage thought, 'Ooh, I'm gonna be a white, soul girl.' You know, the album genuinely did just come together very naturally and very organically."

▲ Adele on *Saturday Night Live* in October 2008, a performance that made swathes of American music fans fall in love with her.

◀ Performing on stage with India.Arie at the VH1 Divas gig at the Brooklyn Academy of Music, New York, in September 2009.

She was adamant, however, that she would never go down the traditional popstar route of making commercially-driven throwaway tracks. She said, "You know, I hate, I'm actually offended by literal easy lyrics that have no thought behind them and are purely written because they rhyme. So I do always want my lyrics to be mature and thoughtful. And, while I've personally now stopped listening to my album because I sing it every day, ultimately I do think it is sincere. Apart from 'Hometown Glory', 'Daydreamer' and 'My Same' – which were all written earlier, when I was between 16 and 18 – the whole album is all about one boy. So I was very sad when I wrote it. And I think that genuinely does come through in the music."

The media loves to define new artists by comparing them to others, and as Adele had joined a musical landscape featuring, as people kept pointing out, three 'Amys' (Winehouse, MacDonald and Duffy – albeit she spelled her name Aimee), two 'Kates' (Tunstall and Nash) and one Lily Allen, she couldn't hide from the comparisons. Un-precious Adele fielded the constant questions about whether she'd turn out like Amy Winehouse, or whether she could beat Duffy in the charts, with grace. However, while only having good things to say about her peers, she was quick to point out that just because they shared a gender didn't mean they should be clumped together into one easy-to-digest group.

Her pleas fell on deaf ears to begin with and when the early reviews of *19* began to pour in, comparisons were par for the course, sometimes positive, sometimes negative. One thing that also became apparent was that there was cynicism over Adele having been awarded the BRITs Critics' Choice Winner award before she'd released an album – it heralded a mini-backlash against her in the music-critic community. She wasn't immune to it. She had herself been baffled by the win and was uncomfortable with the pressure it brought – though she would only admit that a year down the line. "The release of Adele Adkins' debut album seems less like a launch than a coronation," wrote the *Guardian's* Dorian Lynskey. "Not content with anointing her the BBC's Sound of 2008, industry pundits seem to have invented a 'Brit,' the Critics' Choice award, solely for her benefit," he wrote.

◀ Looking svelte and chic at the CMT Artists of the Year Awards in 2010. It was to be one of only a handful of public appearances Adele made in that year.

"Next to [Amy Winehouse's] *Back to Black's* Tanqueray-strength heartache, *19* is more of an alcopop." Priya Elan in the *New Musical Express* wrote, "For all the hype, Adele is not yet ready to produce an album of sufficient depth to match her voice." However, he conceded she could still prove him wrong. "Popular wisdom holds that Winehouse didn't hit her stride until after her debut: perhaps that's the case with Adele."

Fortunately there were more than enough reviews at the opposite end of the spectrum to keep her smiling. Some were positively glowing. Referring to Winehouse, MacDonald, Allen and Duffy, Caspar Llewellyn Smith of the *Observer* said Adele "might be the best of the bunch." He awarded *19* five stars and summed up his sparkling review with, "Think Dusty or Aretha, albeit of SW2 [the area post code for Brixton in London] ... *19* has been on repeat for several weeks now and I suspect will be for the rest of the year." *BBC Music* wrote, "Her melodies exude warmth, her singing is occasionally stunning and, in the dramatic 'Hometown Glory', the spiky cool of 'Cold Shoulder' (which is unexpectedly reminiscent of Shara Nelson-era Massive Attack) and the piano epic 'Make You Feel My Love', she has tracks that make Lily Allen and Kate Nash sound every bit as ordinary as they are." *Billboard* threw its full weight behind the collection, predicting that Adele had "the potential to become among the most respected and inspiring international artists of her generation."

The signs were all pointing in the right direction. When *19* was finally released on January 28, 2008, it went straight to No. 1. You can imagine Adele breathing a huge sigh of relief: she had thumbed her nose at the cynics and delivered on her promise – all in time for the BRIT Awards. She was a jumble of feelings ahead of picking up her BRIT Critics' Choice award: excited, jubilant, nervous, and a tiny bit concerned that people still thought she hadn't done enough to deserve it. She needn't have been worried. When she attended the glittering music show on February 20, the arena was full of good feeling for her – plus *19* had been sitting pretty at the album top spot for several weeks. It was to be a big night out for Adele. The previous year she'd watched the show from her couch, with a record deal to her name, but no inspiration, and

▶ Adele in 2008, sporting a more mature and sophisticated look than she had before.

**Next page (left):** Adele launched her career at the beginning of 2008, as did Welsh singer Duffy. The media had a field day pitching the two singers against one another.

**Next page (right):** Lily Allen had been paving the way for feisty female singers for a couple of years before Adele hit the scene. The stand-no-nonsense chanteuses inevitably drew comparisons.

the year before that she'd watched it from the crowd pit at the front of the stage along with her fellow BRIT School classmates. She decided to dress accordingly, of course. In an interview with the *Sun*, before the show, she promised, "I'm getting to wear diamonds, real ones. Big ones. I'm used to Argos's Elizabeth Duke [an inexpensive brand of jewellery] range myself!"

On the night of the awards, she was as sparkly as her gems. She won journalists over on the red carpet, went star-spotting backstage, performed Coldplay's 'God Put a Smile on My Face' as part of a Mark Ronson medley, (also featuring Daniel Merriweather and Amy Winehouse) and then accepted her BRIT award from none other than Will Young, who looked genuinely happy to be the one doing the presenting. "It gives me so much pleasure," he beamed, "so please give a big cheer to the gorgeous Adele." She came on stage giggling. Dressed in a 60s'-style tunic and leggings, her hair pulled into a side bun, she was showing off the big, glittering earrings she'd promised herself. She gave Will a big hug and then started her speech with, "Erm … hiya," before

◄ ▲ In these black-and-white shots Adele channels old-school glamour and looks quite the timeless star. These publicity photographs were taken in Paris, France, in 2008.

making a little joke about the amount of time that had passed since being named the winner of the inaugural award and being presented with it. "I'm not going to speak for too long because I think speeches are really boring, but I wanted to say thank you to a few people." She thanked her fans, her manager, Alison Howe of *Later with Jools Holland* and, of course, "My beautiful mum." She hinted that receiving the award was a bit of a burden, but now she had collected it, it was like a weight off of her shoulders. "I'm glad, there's been so much hype about it. But I'm like 'Yeah, I've got it now. Shut up!'" she said after the show.

Now that was out of the way, Adele could get on with promoting the record, but despite landing a BRIT award and a No. 1 album on her own merit, she was still dealing with the Winehouse and Duffy comparisons. She didn't let it get to her. Instead, illustrating a kind of twenty-first century-girl-power, she pledged her support to them. "I love all the girls that are out right now. I love Amy. I think Duffy's great. I'm a huge fan of theirs. I buy their albums, I go to their shows. The only time it gets annoying is when they run an article about me and put a picture of Amy with it too," she said. In spite of her well-documented problems, Adele held Winehouse up as an inspiration, claiming she loved her first album, that the follow-up was "phenomenal" and the third, which was sadly never to be, would be even better. "It's exactly that kind of longevity that I want," she said. "Then as far as comparisons with those girls in general go, I think I'm less of a product, and there's probably less to buy into with me. I don't have a style, I'm not a fashionista. With me it's just music, and I don't think I'm as quirky as the others."

As inevitable as the comparisons to the other artists with whom she shared a sex, came the scrutiny of her 'look.' Adele had never been a pipsqueak. Standing at a statuesque 5'9", she had always been a size 14 or 16, sometimes going up to a size 18. She was by no means the archetypal doll-sized popstar of the dreams of music men in 'grey suits,' and photo shoots were definitely not her favourite thing. She took it all in stride though, being happy that she didn't fit the traditional female

**Previous pages:** Adele performing for the VH1 Divas concert, looking stylish in trademark black dress.

▶ As 2008 turned into 2009, hair was swept to the side, Adele's kohl-rimmed eyes looked sultry and there was even a hint of bling.

▲ This 2008 shot of Adele performing at that year's Montreux Jazz Festival shows just how much of an image change she underwent during the *19* album campaign.

◀ Adele on the red carpet at the 2009 Black Ball in New York, where she performed on the same bill as her heartthrob, Justin Timberlake.

popstar mould, and so did her fans. The fact that she looked like a regular girl *and* possessed a voice of spine-tingling power was part-and-parcel of her magic. With her long, auburn hair, feline green eyes, full lips and curves, there was no denying she was gorgeous, but in an approachable way – the kind of girl both guys and girls would be happy to approach down at the pub for a chat, and fall a little bit in love with. In a way, she was just like us, and what was refreshing was that she wasn't afraid to defend herself against the perceived notion of beauty or to tell the world that she was happy with herself.

A fresh, new female role-model, she said, "I didn't make music to become a sex-symbol. I make music to inspire people and make a good record and be part of the music industry. To me, the image isn't part of music. Music is in your ears, not your eyes." She was prepared for the microscopic gaze focused on her figure, however. "I knew people would ask me – especially [in the US] with the whole Hollywood thing – if I felt pressure to lose weight. I don't think it is important. I think it used to be more important, and I think there are aspects of it now where people will talk about what you look like. I made a record. I don't want to be on the front cover of *Playboy*. I want to be on the front cover of *Rolling Stone* with my clothes on."

And yet still the questions came. 'Did she feel pressure to lose weight to find a man?' was one of the tabloids' favourites. "If my husband called me fat, I'd murder him," she said. Did she feel pressure to be reed-thin a la Winehouse? "I'm just not bothered. It doesn't bother me," she countered. It was getting exhausting. "I'm not naïve, I don't believe I need to look like that. I'm very confident, even when I read people saying horrible stuff about my weight," she affirmed. "Until I start not liking my own body, until it gets in the way of my health or stops me having a boyfriend then I don't care. I'm fine."

And it was just that kind of sass and self-confidence that would help her crack the notoriously tricky US market. On that front, in early 2008, things were looking very positive, her tracks having already been picked up and used on mainstream TV shows, creating an online buzz. Music lovers on the other side of the pond were keen to hear more of the London lass with the killer pipes, and in March 2008 she signed a joint venture deal with XL and Columbia Records in the States to tour the country. She went over there that month and did the radio and TV rounds, following it up with a mini-tour of the UK. She then went back to the States where she played über-cool venues such as Joe's Pub in Manhattan – the scene of Amy Winehouse's American live debut – which were triumphs that prepared US fans for the June release of *19*.

At the end of May, she embarked on a world tour called 'An Evening With Adele,' starting in North America and taking in numerous dates across the country, before heading out to Europe in June and July, followed by a whistle-stop tour of London. After that she was set to fly back out to America and tour well into 2009. The tour got off to a good start and the US fans loved what they saw. They were entranced by the girl with the filthy mouth and voice of an angel, often squealing with laughter at her gigs, and what with the accompanying radio and TV Adele was doing, momentum was beginning to grow. Duffy was doing well in the States too, but there was something about Adele that the American audiences really warmed to, her universal R&B-tinged tunes, maybe, and her unerring frankness and sweet vulnerability on stage.

However, despite the plaudits, Adele was about to disappoint them. In August, she announced she was axing the rest of the US tour. In a statement, she said: "There are some problems at home that I've had to stay and sort out, and at the moment they're stopping me from being away for any long period of time. I was really looking forward to touring again and throwing myself back into it all. But my home life needs more attention right now. I apologize from the bottom of my heart for disappointing you all, I'm truly gutted."

It was the first sign that the pressure was getting to her. The adulation had showed no signs of drying up, after all. After the BRITs, Adele was nominated for more awards: Best Jazz Act at the Urban Music Awards (which she won), the *Q* magazine Best Breakthrough Act (which she didn't win) and Best UK Female

at the MOBOs. And she wasn't always comfortable with it. The full story behind the cancellation of the tour didn't emerge until a year later, when she confessed she had been going through an 'E.L.C.' – aka an 'early life crisis.'

The truth was Adele was feeling the pressure of all her 'hype.' She was just an ordinary girl who didn't eat out at fancy restaurants ("I tried the Ivy and it was rubbish," she said in a newspaper interview) or spend her downtime schmoozing and designer clothes shopping. In 2008, she was sick of feeling as if she were missing out on her friends' and her own life. So she gave herself a break, had fun with her friends and happened to meet a guy – a man she believed, back then, was 'The One.' Fast-forward a year to June 2009, and she would admit to a journalist from *Nylon* magazine, "I was drinking far too much and that was kind of the basis of my relationship with this boy. I couldn't bear to be without him, so I was like, 'Well, OK, I'll just cancel my stuff then …. I can't believe I did that …. It seems so ungrateful."

Summer 2008 was to be the singer's 'lost period.' Notably, she bought her own pad in Notting Hill, which she loved because it reminded her of one of her favourite films, and which she moved into in November. She spent the summer in pubs and beer gardens, attending boozy barbeques and picnics with her mates and her new man, and getting away from the glare of publicity. She smoked too many cigs, drank too much red wine and ignored her phone bills (she later had her mobile phone cut off, which she admitted wouldn't have happened if she had been living with Penny). But she couldn't hide away completely. Adele might have decided to turn her back on fame, but fame didn't turn its back on her. In June it was announced that *19* had been nominated for the prestigious British Nationwide Mercury Prize. She didn't win – that accolade went to indie band Elbow – but to be picked out alongside the likes of Radiohead and Laura Marling was a boon for Adele.

The States didn't turn their back on her either. She might have cancelled her tour but she was given a second chance. In October 2008, she received a call from the producers of *Saturday Night Live*. They wanted her to perform two songs on the show, including

◄ Looking glamourous in black and white: in the studio with her mic in July 2009.

'Chasing Pavements', which had been featured on even more TV soundtracks by now. As if that weren't enough of a coup, there was something else. The then-vice US presidential candidate and publicity-magnet Sarah Palin had been booked to appear on the same show. The hype around Palin's appearance was huge, and it was predicted that record numbers of viewers would tune in. Predictions were correct: a record 17 million people watched the show and saw Adele perform 'Chasing Pavements' and 'Cold Shoulder'. The country liked what it heard.

As soon as the show was over, her singles and album sales surged. *19* shot to the top of the iTunes chart, reached number 5 on Amazon and eventually hit No. 11 on the *Billboard* chart, while 'Chasing Pavements' shot to No. 25 on the *Billboard* Top 100. By February 2009, *19* was certified gold in the States. It had been a surreal night for Adele, not least when Palin introduced herself and told her she was a big fan. Not one to be overly impressed by power, the eternally honest Adele said, "I thought she was very funny on the show and she was really nice backstage," before adding, "I don't like her politics. I think she's a lunatic."

Adele's *SNL* appearance saw her status as 'next big thing' cemented in the States. However, the sometime-reluctant star was still finding several aspects of her fame a little hard to adjust to. In an end-of-year interview with the *Guardian* she admitted the worst bit about fame was "Drugs. Coke is everywhere. It would be so easy to fall into it. I am an addictive personality: if I start something I don't stop. I smoke 30 cigarettes a day. I drank a lot in the past. I know I would go on to other things and I don't want that. A close family member died from heroin so I'm frightened of it." And in an interview with the *Telegraph*, she admitted that her BRIT award was an albatross around her neck. "I was scared the Critics' Choice was going to jinx it, and I think that it has in some ways – because it made me seem like a product, and I think I'm the least of a product of everyone out there. But again, it gave me leverage to do really well." It had indeed. 2008 was hugely successful for Adele, but she still had more to achieve.

And so the stage was set for a fairy tale start to the New Year, not that she had any inclination of how it was set to explode.

It was January 2009, and the eternally humble singer was at home, surfing the web to see how many Grammys her British contemporaries were up for, when she discovered something that made her jaw hit the floor. She had been nominated for four Grammys herself. She recalled, "I was told I was a long shot for the Grammys, so I forgot to tell Mum the night the nominations were being announced. I went online to see how many Leona Lewis got – I'm a big fan – and it was 'Adele, Adele, Adele, Adele'. I never thought in my wildest dreams with my first record that I'd be included."

*"I went online to see how many [Grammys] Leona Lewis got – I'm a big fan – and it was 'Adele, Adele, Adele, Adele.' I never thought in my wildest dreams (with my first record) that I'd be included."*

She was nominated for Song of the Year, Best Female Pop Vocal Performance and Record of the Year for 'Chasing Pavements', along with Best New Artist – alongside Duffy, whom despite outselling Adele in 2008 and being in Adele's opinion the "sound of 2008," only received three nominations. There was to be another surprise in store. Adele, renowned for her love of loose tunics, leggings and the odd splurge in a discount store, received a call from none other than Anna Wintour, US *Vogue* editor-in-chief and general all-round style empress, who wanted to dress her for the bash. Anna called on the services of her designer friend Barbara Tfank, who worked with Adele closely on a gorgeous, noir-ish '50s' number, all nipped-in waist and lush textures – in Adele's trademark black. On the night of the ceremony, Adele's hair was backcombed into a side-swept seriously stylish bouffant, while her green eyes were given a sooty, sultry makeover.

Adele's million-dollar look didn't go unnoticed. All eyes

were on the Tottenham girl and expectations were high. When she performed 'Chasing Pavements', the room crackled with excitement. And yet she was so completely oblivious to the spell she had cast over everyone in the audience, and in the States in general, that she hadn't even taken her beloved mum Penny along with her – because she didn't think she would win anything. Of course, she was proved wrong. Delivering on all her heart-palpitating promise, Adele won two of the prestigious awards – one for Best New Artist, in which she beat Duffy and pop sensations Jonas Brothers – and the other for Best Female Pop Vocal Performance.

After the ceremony, Kevin Jonas told MTV, "Adele … she's only like one of the best artists ever. It's cool." To say Adele was surprised and emotional was an understatement. With a wobble in her voice, she punctuated her thank-you speech with, "I think I'm gonna cry." After the ceremony she told journalists that she was most looking forward to getting out of her Spanx and having a cigarette and a glass of red wine with her team. You had to love her.

*"I didn't make music to become a sex-symbol. I make music to inspire people and make a good record, and be part of the music industry. To me, the image isn't part of music. Music is in your ears, not your eyes."*

Her Grammy success took a while to sink in, but eventually she got her head around it – and had the trophies to prove it. Likening the night to an out-of-body experience, she said, "I was literally hovering above myself, laughing. It was just ridiculous to be nominated, like a secret members club that not many Brits get invited to. I was completely unprepared. I had gum in my mouth, my shoes were off, I was texting underneath my chair. But it was

◄ Looking fresh-faced and smiley in early 2009 ahead of her double Grammy Award win.

the most amazing night off my entire life. Every time I get up in the morning I'm reminded of it when I go into my dining room and there are my Grammys. It was the turning point, so electric, I could feel it when I was there that if I did a good job my career could turn around."

The rest of 2009 was a whirlwind of successes, dreams realized and scintillating live shows. She met her idol Beyoncé. She received a congratulatory letter from the then-British prime minister Gordon Brown, praising her for bringing feel-good cheer to Britain amidst the recession. She made a guest-appearance on *Ugly Betty*. She did a month's unpaid work in London's Rough Trade record store to reconnect herself with music and reality, which she loved ("I just did it for myself, they were baffled I volunteered to do it"). She got herself a dog, a male miniature dachshund, whom she'd wanted to call Britney, but who, at the eleventh hour, got his reprieve after howling along to a Louis Armstrong record, and became Louie (with an 'e'). She spent her twenty-first birthday on stage at the Rosewood Ballroom in New York where her mum turned up with a huge cake. She met her crush, Justin Timberlake ("I wanted to say, 'I love you, let's get married and have children,' but instead I just barked at him, woof. I always bark at boys when I fancy them"). She performed alongside Kelly Clarkson, Leona Lewis and India.Arie in VH1's Diva show. And as her mum prepared to turn 40 – a landmark age – this got Adele thinking about how much her mum had done for her and how happy she was to be able to repay her. "In a way, my success has been for her," she said in an interview with the *Daily Mail*. "Mum loves me being famous. She is so excited and proud, as she had me so young and couldn't support me, so I am living her dream. It's sweeter for both of us."

The whole year could have been a dream come true if it weren't for one thing: the end of an earth-shaking, heart-breaking relationship.

▶ In stark contrast to her evolving sophisticated diva image, an early 19 publicity shot: a riot of colour, and pattern.

# 5

# Superstardom: *21*

Adele had promised her fans she wouldn't go back into the studio until she had something to write about. That something was the end of a relationship so inspiring and significant it sparked a seismic shift in her view of the world. She was 21, he was older. He opened her eyes to travel, wine, literature and art. They had had it all, and then it ended. The drama of the breakup and subsequent tremors were the subject of album two, *21* – a momentous age in more ways than one.

The relationship had changed her. She had matured and now felt more like a woman than a girl. "*19* was all about a relationship but the relationship I had at 21 was more intense," she said. "It was all or nothing, we did everything together, it was no longer me, him, or I. It was us, we, them, they." He changed her in a million ways, she said. But then it fell apart. "We fell out of love, it was devastating," she explained. "Unlike my first boyfriend who cheated on me, this time we just stopped loving each other and I felt like a complete failure. He was the love of my life and it was bad timing."

Angry, hurt, shocked and generally in pieces, Adele started writing the album at the end of 2009, and spent much of 2010 in the studio getting it out of her system. A broken heart had never sounded so tuneful, but little did she know at the time how monumental this was to be. The precursor to the album was the

▶ Back with a vengeance and a new album – the hair was longer, the lashes thicker, the "look" and sound more iconic.

▲ ▶ The success of *21* meant Adele sold out venues all over the United States, such as the Beacon Theatre, New York, in 2011, after which she received rave reviews.

single 'Rolling in the Deep'. Released on November 29, 2010, it was a funky, thundering kiss-off, produced by Florence + The Machine producer Paul Epworth. The sonic equivalent of her slamming a stiletto heel to the pavement in fury, it heralded her return to the scene with a bang louder than any firework that had gone off that month. 'I'm back and you'd better listen to me,' it seemed to say. Over a thumping beat and a stomping piano, the singer laid down a dark, disco-gospel track with razor-sharp lyrics. It's the sound of a scorned lover, hell-bent on revenge. Throughout the track she threatens to wreak devastating emotional consequences on her retreating ex-lover. Yet, as the chorus that was to blare out from millions of radios across the globe made clear, they could have had it all. The powerful accompanying video shows Adele in profile, her hair pulled up into a '60s' bouffant, while glasses of water shake, plates smash and belongings burn. The imagery is stark. She had made her point.

And it was a game-changer. On its release it went straight to No. 2 in the UK charts, and while it might not have made the top spot, its genre-straddling sound meant it dominated radio playlists from Radio 1 to Magic FM. 'Rolling in the Deep' became a monster hit, not just in the UK but in the rest of Europe, Canada and Australasia. It was to be a fixture in the UK Top 10 for months and months to come, while its release in the States would herald a stellar turn to Adele's career. It strutted fabulously into the *Hot 100*, sashayed to the No. 1 spot and dug its heels into it long enough for it be crowned the biggest-selling single of 2011. But that was yet to come.

"It's me saying, 'Get the f**k out of my house,' instead of me begging him to come back," explained Adele. "It's my reaction to being told my life was going to be boring and lonely and rubbish, and that I was a weak person if I didn't stay in a relationship. I wrote it as a sort of 'f**k you.'" All that darkness and melodrama was not just a product of clever lyrics and production wizardry. Adele wrote the track when angry and tearful, the day after the breakup. Epworth recalled, "She was obviously quite fragile and very open about what had happened. But she had fire in her belly." The expression "roll deep" is British slang for 'I've got your back.' It had a double-edged meaning of course: now she had broken up with him, Adele didn't feel like anyone had her back. She was adamant she would release the track as her first single, but realized it was gamble, as it was such a different sounding record. "I wanted to be a bit more bluesy, which I needed a bigger production for. And off-record I'm a bit more sarcastic and funny and I wanted that to come across," she said. "I feel a lot bolder now, I wanted a bit of 'oomph' behind (the songs)."

*"19 was all about a relationship but the relationship I had at 21 was more intense."*

It was Adele like we had never heard her before. It was obvious this man had had a massive impact on her. "He made me an adult. He put me on the road that I'm traveling on," she told *Rolling Stone*. "Most of my life was my career, but I had this little side project that was us. And it made me feel really normal again, which is just what I needed. Because I was becoming a bit doolally – a bit f**kin' crazy." He lived with her for almost a year at her Notting Hill flat before things began to slide. "It just stopped being fun," she said. "He was artistic, but not romantic."

Adele recorded parts of 'Rolling in the Deep' in London with Paul Epworth, and Fraser T. Smith – famous for his work with the likes of James Morrison – and in L.A. with OneRepublic's Ryan Tedder – who wrote and produced Leona Lewis's 'Bleeding Love' and Beyoncé's 'Halo'. She also recorded in Malibu with legendary producer and Columbia Records co-founder Rick Rubin at his Shangri-La studio. The album *21* is Adele's coming-of-age record, jam-packed with rich new sounds and gutsy, grown-up lyrics. 'Rolling in the Deep' was the perfect album opener, a feisty mission statement.

It is followed in the track listing by 'Rumour Has It'. Produced by Tedder, whom Adele had met in a hotel elevator after the 2009 Grammys, it's another bluesy-pop stomp and full of '60s'

▲ Performing on NBC's *Today* show
in February 2011.

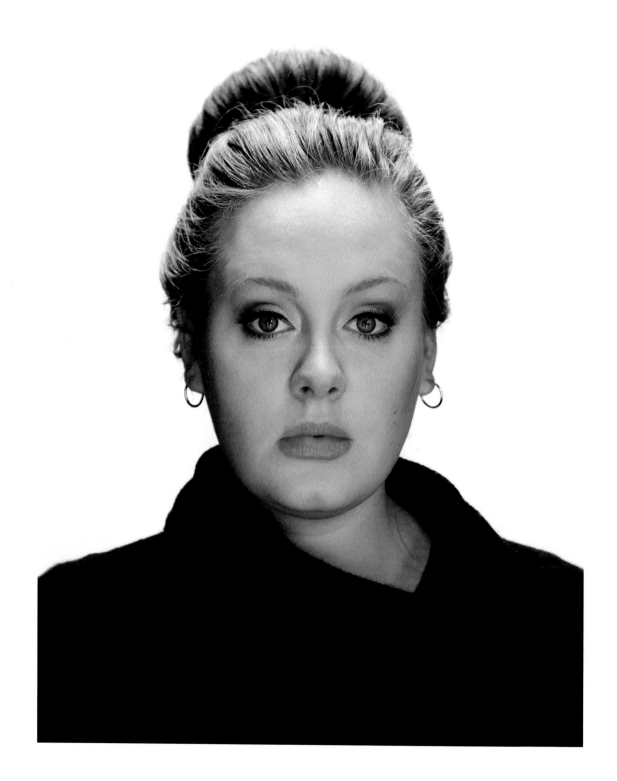

girl group sass. Surprisingly, the track is not about Adele's man, but about her friends back home, who'd become gluttons for the gossip mags. "I'd catch up with my friends and they'd be like, 'I heard you're seeing blah, blah.' My own friends were gossiping about me! It's about my own friends believing what they hear and me being mortified. But it's very sarcastic and tongue-in-cheek."

Tedder was astounded by how easy Adele made the recording

*"It's my reaction to being told my life was going to be boring and lonely and rubbish, and that I was a weak person if I didn't stay in a relationship."*

process look. "She sang it once top to bottom, pitch perfect, she didn't miss a note. I looked at the engineer then at her and said, 'Adele, I don't know what to tell you but I have never had anyone do that in ten years.' Putting a vocal on typically takes around four or five hours to make perfect, she did it in one take," he says.

Ryan Tedder also produced the next song on the album. 'Turning Tables' is archetypal Adele – an atmosphere-drenched torch song. With its swirling swings and plaintive piano, it sounds like the big sister of 'Hometown Glory', but thematically, is quite different. It was written in the wake of a huge bust-up with her ex, while they were still together. When Adele caught up with Tedder in the studio she told him she was sick of her boyfriend turning the tables on her in arguments. An idea for a song title was hatched.

'Don't You Remember', produced by Rick Rubin, comes next, signalling a complete sonic departure for Adele. It's a track steeped in the atmosphere of country music – the sounds of which she'd listened to and absorbed while recording the album in the States. While on tour in the American Deep South, the driver of her tour bus introduced her to contemporary Nashville music.

**Previous pages:** In Los Angeles at a photo shoot for *Elle* magazine, July 2009.

◄ At a photo shoot for AOL, 2011.

"He listened to all this amazing country music and we'd rock out late at night, chain smoking and listening to Rascal Flatts," she told *Spin* magazine. He inspired her to check out the back catalogues of Dolly Parton, Garth Brooks and Steel River. She spent four-and-a-half intense weeks at Rubin's famed studio in Malibu, California – an experience that had a massive impact on her. "He's amazing. It's all about the songs, all about the music," she said of Rubin. However, the experience wasn't 100 percent problem-free. And during the month she spent in Malibu, Adele experienced waves of homesickness. She looked on the bright side, of course. "It was so isolating in the studio but in a really great way," she said. "We just vibed until it felt right and there was no referencing of things in the charts that were doing well or whatever, no seeing what was hot and what was not, and there are no samples used at all. I could sit here now and play the entire record completely live without any electricity. It was just so organic."

The track also signalled a change in mood from restrained rage to reflectiveness. With minimal production and her voice the focal point, 'Don't You Remember' was clearly aimed at the huge and lucrative country music market in the States. It was the final song Adele recorded for the album at a time when she was feeling more philosophical about her failed relationship and the future. She explained, "I started remembering what it was that I actually loved about my ex, and at the beginning I'd have a panic attack if he didn't text me back within 10 seconds of me texting him. And I always dwell on stuff, which that lyric is about. I find it really hard to move on sometimes, which is something that I'm only just realizing, it's something I need to work on."

Power ballad 'Set Fire to the Rain' came next and very much lived up to its title. A thundering, glossily produced track with verses rising to a big crashing crescendo of a chorus, and strings that swelled and burst like a musical thunder storm. Some critics deemed it "melodramatic" and said Adele sounded better when backed by just a piano or guitar. Nonetheless, it had 'radio hit' stamped all over it. Produced and co-written with Fraser T. Smith, it's about knowing you need to let go of an unhealthy

relationship but not being strong enough to do it.

'He Won't Go', also produced by Rubin and co-written with Fraser T. Smith, sees Adele change musical direction again. A slinky R&B-flavoured track, it recalls the style of one of her teen idols, Mary J. Blige, and is about knowing a relationship isn't right but wanting to take an extra gamble on it, nevertheless. Next track, 'Take It All', was the first song she wrote for *21*. Adele was still with her ex when she wrote it and she even played it to him. She jokes now that the relationship ended shortly afterwards ("he was an a**ehole and I was a bitch – it was never meant to be"), but it's still one of the hardest songs on the album for her to sing.

The bluesy, upbeat 'I'll Be Waiting' – the second track produced by Paul Epworth – followed, and offered a slice of optimism. Despite painting a picture of a tumultuous relationship, the chorus was perky. The romantic, old soul sound of 'One and Only' heard her channelling Aretha Franklin, with echoes of '(You Make Me Feel) Like A Natural Woman'. She wrote it in the early stages of an old relationship, before her life-changing ex. She said, "I wrote it when I was really happy and I was like, 'Woo, I've got it in me to write a happy song,' but then when I got with the guy who the song's about, he was a f**king bastard..."

Track eleven is a reworking of the Cure's 'Lovesong' – the soundtrack to one of her first and happiest memories: the time her mum took her to see the Cure live in Finsbury Park when she was just a toddler. She recorded it in one take with Rubin, giving it a bossa nova lilt. The results are touching. She admitted, "I'm really sad in it 'cause I'm missing home. The whole experience of being in Malibu in Rick Rubin's studio was a bit overwhelming really. Amazing ... but I felt a bit heavy and that song set me free a bit. I sang it for my mum. My voice had gone a bit which I was paranoid about but it really suits the song."

For Rubin – who has worked with such musical luminaries as the Beastie Boys, Tom Petty, Mick Jagger and Johnny Cash, working with Adele was a magical experience. Talking about the recording of 'Lovesong', he told industry magazine *M*, "Her singing was so strong and heartbreaking in the studio, it was clear something very special was happening. The musicians were inspired as they rarely get to play with the artist present, much less singing. Today, most things are recorded as overdubs on track. This was truly an interactive moment where none of the musicians knew exactly what they were going to play and all were listening so, so, deeply and completely to figure out where they fitted in. All of the playing was keying off the emotion on Adele's outrageous vocal performance."

*"It was so isolating in the studio but in a really great way, we just vibed until it felt right ..."*

The final song on the album is one that has reached iconic status. 'Someone Like You' needs no introduction. Over a simple piano melody, Adele sings a heart-breaking ode to her ex who has moved on and found a new girlfriend. She kind-of gives him and his new partner her blessing, while making a dig (subtly but significantly) about finding someone herself and sounding vulnerable and strong at the same time. DJ Zane Lowe once said of Adele, Her voice is a direct conduit between who she is and what we hear, there's nothing that gets in the way." And that sentiment is nowhere more evident than in this song. Anyone who has gone through a painful breakup could relate to the conflicting, horribly raw emotions Adele expressed. For many, it was as if she was singing their experience as much as her own.

She wrote the song after receiving a text from one of her and her ex's mutual friends informing her that her ex had got engaged. Despite the relationship having been over for a while and Adele feeling as if she were over the worst, the news was shattering. She turned the taps on a bath and while waiting for it to run, wrote the track lying on her bed, sobbing. The sentiment couldn't be more opposite to opening track 'Rolling in the Deep'. While that track was a defiant I'll be just fine without you," in 'Someone Like You' she sounded bereft, yet dignified. She believes it's the best

◀ Adele at the MTV Video Music Awards in Los Angeles, in August 2011, where her videos bagged her three pieces of silverware.

▼ Performing for BBC Radio 1's famous *Live Lounge* show, with host Fearne Cotton in January 2011.

song she has ever written. She worked on the simple arrangement alongside songwriter Dan Wilson, old-school-style with just a piano. "The relationship that the entire record is about is really summed up in 'Someone Like You'," she said on its release. "I can imagine being about 40 and looking for him again and turning up and he's settled and he's got a beautiful wife and some beautiful kids and he's completely happy and I'm still on my own. It's kind of about that and I'm quite scared about that."

And yet writing the song was cathartic, her therapy. In an interview with *Rolling Stone*, she said light-heartedly, "I wrote that song because I was exhausted from being such a bitch.... And when I did it, I felt so freed." It was released on the same day as the album, which followed on from where *19* left off by soaring straight to the top of the UK album charts.

As with *19*, its reviews spanned the spectrum from slightly sniffy to stuffed full of superlatives. Will Dean of the *Guardian* surmised that it was a "progressive, grown-up second collection," and that it would ensure "Adele is around for [albums entitled] 23, 25, 27 and beyond." He described 'Someone Like You' as gorgeous. "It's nearly good enough reason to break up with someone, simply so you can mope in it." Kitty Empire of the *Observer* worried the album sounded a little too American. "If you take the girl out of Brixton, do you take the grit out of the girl?" she pondered. But she too loved 'Someone Like You'. "More of this bunny-boiling intensity wouldn't go amiss on an album where the shivers don't come as often as they should," she said. The *NME* gave the album a disappointing four out ten, extolling the virtues of 'Rolling in the Deep' and 'Rumour Has It', but despairing of the "pastel-pink mush" of much of the rest of the album. The BBC's review was shining, however. "*21* is simply stunning," wrote Ian Wade. "It will see Adele become an even greater award-magnet come the end of the year, leaving her contemporaries for dust. Genuinely brilliant."

That it did, and with its eclectic mix of country, blues, soul, pop, R&B and funk, it was to become a genuine crossover hit – played as much on the UK's Radio 1 as it was on Radio 2. It would also become a staple of country, pop, *and* R&B radio

stations in the States – the Holy Grail of any artist wanting to smash America. But that was way off yet.

Nevertheless, bagging her second UK No. 1 album you'd imagine would be all the incentive Adele needed to grab a bunch of mates, hit the pub and celebrate her achievement with a bucket-load of red wine. She wasn't able to celebrate at all, however. In what was to become a recurring illness throughout the year, Adele had been laid low with laryngitis, a condition which singers with voices as big as hers are particularly prone to. "It was so frightening," she revealed. "I stopped smoking, drinking, eating or drinking citrus, spicy foods and caffeine. It was so f\*\*king boring. When my album went No. 1 here and in America I just sat in my room and watched telly 'cause I couldn't go out and talk to anyone."

She might have been battling a nasty infection, but her condition improved enough in time for her performance at the 2011 BRIT Awards at London's O2 Arena. If there were issues with her voice, she hid them and ended up delivering a performance so spellbinding that her status moved from successful pop star to global sensation in the space of four minutes. Rather than singing the pacey 'Rolling in the Deep', she chose to perform 'Someone Like You', a song that was yet to set the singles chart alight in the UK. All things said and done, it was a bit of a gamble. And yet there was something in the air that suggested it was going to be a remarkable performance. When she did appear, she was dressed in her trademark understated black, with just a piano and pianist for company. As she began to sing, a hush descended on the audience. It was a performance of incredible power, each painful, deeply personal line, reflected in her facial expressions. She looked both a picture of strength and vulnerability on stage. As the song drew to a close, a cloud of glittering ticker-tape fluttered to the floor and Adele's eyes filled up. Wiping her eyes, she stood smiling sheepishly, while the audience got to their feet to applaud, many of them brushing 'something' from their own eyes, too. BRITs host, James Corden, was stunned; "Wow," he said, summing up the mood of everyone watching.

After the show, she admitted, "I was really emotional by the

**Previous pages:** Simply breathtaking: Adele's icon status-cementing performance at the BRIT Awards in 2011.

◄ Guffawing in her own loveable way outside the Ed Sullivan Theatre in New York before an appearance on the *David Letterman Show*.

▶ Few artists come close to imbuing their performances with the kind of raw, heartfelt emotion Adele regularly displays. This concert was in August, 2011 at the Xcel Center, Saint Paul, Minnesota.

end because I'm quite overwhelmed by everything anyway, and then I had a vision of my ex, of him watching me at home and he's going to be laughing at me, because he knows I'm crying because of him, with him thinking, 'Yep, she's still wrapped around my finger.' Then everyone stood up, so I was overwhelmed." Adele didn't need special effects, her voice was enough, and the heartfelt lyrics, resonating with anyone who'd ever been in a relationship, brought on a mass lump in the throat. In short, it was an understated phenomenon.

You only need look at what happened in the charts directly after that performance for proof. *21* experienced an 890 per cent sales surge on Amazon.co.uk in the hour after the BRITs broadcast, while her performance racked up millions of YouTube hits. That weekend, 'Someone Like You' leapt from No. 47 to No. 1 in the UK singles chart, while 'Rolling in the Deep'climbed to No. 4. And while *21* held tight to the No. 1 album position chart, *19* surged to No. 4, and then No. 2.

In doing so, Adele became the first living act since the Beatles in 1964 to have two UK top-five albums and singles simultaneously. *21* was to stay at No. 1 for an incredible 11 straight weeks, and kept pop powerhouse Lady Gaga – who had ruled the charts in 2009 and 2010 while Adele was busy recording – from hitting the top spot with her second album *Born This Way.* (Yes, that bang you heard could well have been the sound of that well-known lobster telephone hitting the wall.) Adele also became the first act since the Corrs in 1999 to hold the No. 1 and No. 2 spots in the UK album charts with two different albums. She was quite simply the name on every music-lover's lips.

How funny, and typical of her, that ahead of her life-changing BRITs performance, she said on the red carpet, "I'm sorry it's not a very big production. It's just a song, there's no dance routine. I don't think I could pull it off. Imagine me dancing in these heels, I'd look like your uncle at a wedding."

*21* was released in the US in March 2012 where it went to No. 1 and was to stay there for a staggering length of time. At last Adele had shrugged off the comparisons with her

contemporaries (Duffy's second album, *Endlessly*, was a relative flop, incidentally). And she had proved that she didn't need to use gimmicks, sell sex or starve herself to a size zero to get there. In an interview with *Rolling Stone*, she said, "My life is full of drama, and I don't have time to worry about something as petty as what I look like.... I don't make music for eyes, I make music for ears."

Having overcome her laryngitis by spring, it was time for that music to reach the fans' ears so Adele hit the road again. She kicked off her sold-out *Adele Live* tour in Norway in March 2011, playing much of Europe throughout March and April, and taking in a few UK dates at the end of April, before embarking on the North American leg of the tour in May. During that time came the mind-blowing news that *21* had spent a record 10 consecutive weeks at the top of the UK charts, and in doing so, had usurped Madonna's *Immaculate Collection* record for the title of longest consecutive run at the top of the UK album charts by a female artist. "Oi, Oi. It's amazing! But it goes over my head. It's not like I Google myself or go, 'What are my figures like this week?'" she said. She was the only person downplaying her success. The director of the Official Charts Company, Martin Talbot, said, "She has gone from being a promising young artist, who existed slightly in the slipstream of acts like Duffy, to become the biggest act in the UK by a country mile. To do so well, you've often got to be quite cheesy, but she's the opposite of cheese – she's popular right across the spectrum."

By summer 2011, Adele's profile was so huge, she could have sold out arenas and festivals many times over. However, displaying that trademark single-mindedness and self-assurance, she chose

**Previous pages:** Backed only by a pianist: Adele's career-defining BRIT Awards 2011 appearance.

◄ Nailing it again with a soulful performance in March 2011.

▶ Adele in the spotlight in Munich, Germany in 2011: she's never been one for special effects or raunchy dancers. She lets her breathtaking voice do the work.

to stick with mid-sized venues and theatres, swearing off festivals. "The thought of an audience that big frightens the life out of me. I don't think the music would work either. It's all too slow," she said in an interview with *Q* magazine. "We had three nights on hold at the O$_2$ and I was like 'I won't play a festival. You think I'm gonna play a f**king arena? Are you out of your mind?' I'd rather play 12 years at the Barfly than one night at the O$_2$. So I've made all those decisions and some people are pretty mortified. They think I'm mad."

The audiences at her sold-out Adele Live tour weren't complaining. They loved being so close to the vivacious London lady, and as ever, she was the consummate show-woman on stage – part best friend, part bawdy barmaid and part super shiver-inducing soul star. She cracked jokes, told stories and made eyes water with that voice as she went along. From an observer's point of view, she always looked totally relaxed and in control on stage, it was as if she was merely entertaining a big group of friends. But that couldn't be further from the truth. Adele has battled with crippling stage fright before each and every gig she has played. Her nerves have gotten worse the more popular she's become, she has admitted – and she doesn't relax until she comes off stage. "The nerves would kick in from the moment I woke up," she said. She is super-conscious of the fact that people have spent their hard-earned cash to go and see her, painfully aware of the fact they've committed an evening to her and desperately doesn't want to let anyone down or shatter their expectations. She said, "I'm scared of audiences .... One show in Amsterdam, I was so nervous I escaped out the fire exit. I've thrown up a couple of times. Once in Brussels, I projectile-vomited on someone. I just gotta bear it. But I don't like touring. I have anxiety attacks a lot."

Her defence mechanism is humour. "I try to bust jokes. It does work," she says. Unfortunately, Adele was to be struck by illness on this tour too. Not long after the North American leg of her tour had gotten underway, she contracted laryngitis again. Forced to postpone five dates, she consulted a throat specialist in L.A. and was given some bad news: her infection

was advanced and she would have to give her voice a proper break. She cancelled the rest of her US dates at the beginning of June and was devastated. On her website, she wrote, "I'm really frustrated. I was hoping with a week's rest, I'd be better to sing again straight away. However there is absolutely nothing I can do but take the doctor's advice and rest some more. I'm so sorry." Some fans were annoyed and responded to her posting by telling her to give up smoking. Fortunately, the majority of the loyal 'Adelettes' were full of sympathy and inundated her with "get well" messages.

May and June 2011 were by no means stellar months for Adele in myriad ways. She had also managed to trigger a backlash in the UK after she grumbled about paying taxes in an interview with *Q*. She said, "I'm mortified to have to pay 50 per cent! [While] I use the NHS [National Health Service], I can't use the public transport any more. Trains are always late, most state schools

▲ Understated but expressive, the voice and the feelings shine through on NBC television, February 2011.

◄ The end of her BRIT Awards 2011 performance.

are s\*\*t and I've gotta give you, like, four million quid – are you having a laugh? When I got my tax bill in from *19*, I was ready to go and buy a gun and randomly open fire." Fortunately for Adele, most people saw the comments as naïve rather than arrogant and, as such, the criticism was short-lived and soon brushed away.

She had bigger things to worry about in June, when the tragic news of Amy Winehouse's death broke. Adele was heartbroken. She took to her blog to pen a moving tribute to the singer. Under a headline 'Amy Flies in Paradise,' Adele wrote, "Not many people have it in them to do something they love, simply because they love it. With no fuss and no compromise. But she knew what she was capable of and didn't even need to try. If she wanted to do something she would and if she didn't, she'd say f\*\*k off." She credited the late star with paving the way for her and making people excited about UK music again. She finished, "I don't think she ever realized just how brilliant she was and how important she is, but that just makes her even more charming."

The summer of 2011 featured as many ups as it did downs, however. *21* was nominated for the Mercury Prize, Team Adele topped the *Guardian's* music Power List 100, leaving Simon Cowell eating her dust, she successfully gave up drinking, her songs were performed on the insanely popular TV show *Glee*, she was nominated at the MTV VMAs and there were also rumours Adele would join Beyoncé on stage during her headlining slot at the Glastonbury festival in June. Her laryngitis put a stop to that, of course, but she still got to hang out with her idol when she was invited to Beyoncé's Shepherds Bush concert the evening after the Glasto show.

Adele and Beyoncé met for the first time at the Grammy Awards the previous year and were becoming friends and fully paid-up members of each other's fan clubs, which made the invite even more special. Adele admitted that Beyoncé and her famous alter ego, Sasha Fierce, had even inspired her come up with her own feisty stage doppelganger ... Sasha Carter! She explained that she had her brainwave the first time she met Bey. "I had a full-blown anxiety attack," she said. "Then she popped in looking gorgeous, and said, 'You're amazing! When I listen to you I feel like I'm listening to God.' Can you believe she said that? Later, I went out on the balcony crying hysterically, and I said, 'What would Sasha Fierce do?' That's when Sasha Carter was born."

Adele had been well and truly sprinkled with Beyoncé's fairy dust.... Showing just how far she'd grown in the 'va-va-voom' stakes, she was asked to grace her first-ever *Vogue* magazine cover (she would be seen smouldering on the cover of the UK October issue). She also landed the cover-girl spot in UK *Glamour* magazine's July issue, which tied in nicely with her winning the UK Solo Artist of the Year award at the magazine's annual awards bash for the second year on the trot. In a typically witty, candid and self-deprecating interview, the singer talked about her whirlwind year so far, wanting to date Prince Harry despite once saying she'd never "go out with a ginger," causing a mini-stampede in Primark department store after going in for a shop, her growing love of high fashion (D&G and Burberry) and her unluckiness in love. Still single at that time, she revealed, "I'm not very good at saying how I feel. I think sometimes I come across as a bit blasé, like, 'I wouldn't be upset if you left me.' But I would." A summer of lows but exhilarating highs paved the way for a magnificent comeback gig.

*"I'm not very good at saying how I feel. I think sometimes I come across as a bit blasé, like, 'I wouldn't be upset if you left me.' But I would."*

She resumed her Adele Live tour on September 13, with a concert at London's legendary Royal Albert Hall. Emerging on stage as a silhouette against a white light, and singing 'Hometown Glory', her voice sounded husky, haunting and full of its trademark power. Cheers rang out, mobile phone lights flickered on, and she left a dramatic pause between the first verse and chorus for a curtain to fall and reveal her new '60s' siren hairdo – all long luscious locks – and a stage backdrop of wonky lampshades, an echo of the makeshift stage her mum constructed for the schoolgirl Adele. Once the song ended, she greeted her adoring crowd by hollering, "Albert f**king Hall!" She was in full Sasha Carter mode throughout the show, despite constantly saying she was nervous and regularly sipping on cups of tea. She performed old and new songs – including a rousing 'Turning Tables' backed by a ten-piece string section.

One of the most emotional moments of the night came when Adele paid tribute to Amy Winehouse. She told the audience, "I've been singing this song for her ever since she died because I knew she loved it. I was so inspired by her but she never took it seriously – just how inspired I was by her. She was such a joker and such a lovely girl. And it's just devastating really." She then ordered the whole audience, including everyone in the balconies and boxes to light up their mobile phones, so the hall looked like a sea of stars. Once the whole of the Royal Albert Hall had complied, she smiled, "She can see us now," she said, before adding, "This is 'Make You Feel My Love' for Amy."

*"I was so inspired by her but she never took it seriously – just how inspired I was by her. She was such a joker and such a lovely girl. And it's just devastating really."*

It wasn't to be the only moving moment during her show. She also revealed that she had made friends with the ex again, but assured them there was no chance she was ever getting back with him. He was very happy in his new relationship, she said, adding: "Time is a great healer." She had turned a corner at last, and was ready to start afresh on a new relationship. Introducing her

first encore number, 'Someone Like You', she said, "I'm not bitter any more, I'm proud of him." As the fans sang the final chorus back to her, those famous feline eyes filled up. As she reached the closing bars, the audience on their feet cheering themselves hoarse, she let the tears flow more freely.

She ended the concert on a rousing version of 'Rolling in the Deep', streams of golden glitter billowing into the crowd, while the foundations of the legendary venue shook to the thunderous mass hand clapping. "Royal Albert Hall thanks for making my dream come true," she grinned. It was as if the grand, imposing venue was made for the larger-than-life London diva and her unearthly voice – although what Her Majesty would have thought of her bluer interludes is open to debate.

However, the pattern of dizzy highs and disappointing lows that had thus far tattooed itself on to Adele's 2011 was set to continue. In October, she was forced to cancel the remaining UK dates of her tour after contracting an illness that proved to be career-threatening. Earlier in the year, while doing an interview on a French radio station she had felt something 'pop' in her throat. That something turned out to be a benign polyp on her vocal cord that had hemorrhaged, but still she kept on singing. Until October 2011, that is, when it became apparent she would need to have surgery on the damage and undertake an intensive recuperation period – it was a scary experience.

She took to her website and wrote, "I'm heartbroken and worried to tell you that yet again I'm experiencing problems with my voice. I have absolutely no choice but to recuperate properly and fully, or I risk damaging my voice forever." The tabloid rumour-mill whirred with ever more salacious stories and the fans began to fear Adele's career might be over for good. Keen to put a stop to the stories, her management issued a statement, explaining her condition in clear terms, which fortunately allayed the fans' fears. During the first week of November, Adele underwent laser microsurgery in Massachusetts in the States. Despite being naturally worried, she was in expert hands. Her op was carried out by esteemed US surgeon Dr. Steven Zeitels, who had successfully carried out procedures on the Who's Roger

◄ Channeling an ever bigger bouffant do, Adele late 2011 'look' was pure 60s glamour.

Daltrey and Aerosmith's Steve Tyler, among others.

**Previous pages:** Performing at the Kesselhaus in Munich, Germany, in March 2011.

The operation was a resounding success. That was the good news. The bad news was: the 100-words-per-minute motor-mouth was ordered not to speak for two whole months while her damaged vocal cords healed. "It was hard, I love talking," she later said. Fortunately she found a handy stand-in solution to her muteness – a phone application that spoke for her. And the best bit, it allowed her to swear. "So I'm still really getting my point across," she recalled.

The final months of the year might have been quiet – literally – but not so quiet in other ways. Looking back on 2011 she might have had to pinch herself really hard to believe it all. After hitting the top spot in 26 countries around the globe – including Australia, New Zealand and Canada, where it reached 'Diamond' status – *21* was named the biggest-selling album of the twenty-first century. She had bettered the sales of, amongst others, Amy Winehouse's legendary *Back to Black* – it was also named the first album in UK chart history to reach sales of three million copies in a calendar year. In America it had sold almost six million (over three times that of Lady Gaga's sophomore album, *Born This Way*) and had helped UK artists take their highest share of US album sales in ten years, with albums by Brit artists accounting for an 11.7 per cent share of all albums sold in the US in 2011. She appeared twice in a list of the 2011 Top 10 UK albums sold in the US, with *21* leading the way with 5.8 million sales, while *19* sat in the fourth spot with sales of 850,000. In November, she won three American Music Awards for Favourite Adult Contemporary Artist, Favourite Pop/Rock Female Artist, and Favourite Pop/Rock Album – the first woman to do so. She also won MTV's Song of the Year for 'Rolling in the Deep' and Best UK/ Ireland Act at the MTV Europe Music Awards. Then came the small announcement that she had been nominated for a jaw-dropping record six Grammy Awards at the US ceremony, set to take place the following February. On top of that, she had been named Artist of the Year, and been the recipient of Top Album for *21* and Top Single for 'Rolling in the Deep' in *Billboard* magazine's end-of-year-honours.

And there was something else – she had fallen in love again, with 36-year-old Simon Konecki, an old Etonian, former banker, entrepreneur and CEO of charity Drop4Drop – an organization

that campaigns to provide clean water in poor countries. Singer Ed Sheeran had introduced Konecki to Adele in October and he had been instrumental in keeping her spirits up during her throat-op convalescence. As irony would have it, the same month she met Simon, she was on the front of UK *Vogue* pledging to stay single for the sake of her music. "I get distracted when I've got someone in my life, which I can't afford to do right now," she had said.

It's not hard to see why the couple hit it off – they are both clever, successful and care about charitable causes. Although she's never shouted about it, Adele always asks non-paying attendees at her gigs to make donations to charity and she has urged her followers on her social networking sites to support Drop4Drop. Being that little bit older than Adele, Simon also had the wisdom and experience she looks for in a guy: it was the perfect set-up. Having made his own fortune, gone through a life-changing relationship (he has been married, divorced and has a child with his ex) and come out of the other side, it's fair to say he and Adele are on a pretty level playing field. They spend their free time together like any other couple, going for meals and taking the dog for country walks. Happily for our North London heroine, she appears to have landed herself a good 'un and she couldn't be happier. "I'm in love now, and I love it! It's great." Finally her wish had come true. She had met someone, and in doing so, drawn the curtains on the biggest story in pop of that year: that of Adele, the ex, and his new love.

# 6

# Hello Again: *25*

After all the adulation of her enormously successful 2011 album, *21*, and buoyed by its long-reaching and lingering success – remaining the bestselling album in the world for both 2011 and 2012 – Adele's next career move was unexpected: she disappeared from the spotlight. It was there that she remained, silent on when, and if, she would ever return, going as far as to say, in 2012, "I'm done being a bitter witch," and "I am f\*\*king off for four or five years". And with that, she vanished.

Fast forward three years, to 2015, and Adele is back. But, as she so rightly claims, she never really left us, she just wanted to "take time and live a little bit". She put the brakes on her own career... for the sake of her own career. "I know some people thought I was mad for taking a break," she told the *Observer* in November 2015. "Even I can see it was a bit weird. But I'm glad it happened. I think it was the right thing. It slowed everything down. That didn't mean I didn't stop going to shops, to parks, to museums," Adele said of her disappearance from the spotlight. "I just wasn't *photographed* while doing it." Adele and Simon, a very private couple and rarely photographed together, have worked hard to keep their family life away from the cameras and journalists eager for a salacious Adele exclusive, but not because they hate the constant flashbulbs in their faces (though they do), but because it's the only way for her fans to see that she is remaining true and real to herself, and her music. "Me being photographed in Waitrose is being famous for no reason

▲ Adele receives a standing ovation from the *X Factor* judges after her performance of 'Hello', Deccember 13, 2015.

and that is something that I am not up for and I will not stand for," Adele told *i-D* magazine. "It's not me trying to be anti-famous, I just want to have a real life so I can write records. No one wants to listen to a record from someone that's lost touch with reality. So I live a low-key life… for my fans. In fact, the only thing that's changed since I became famous is that I now shop in Waitrose."

Adele's extended hiatus has helped the singer-songwriter's fame grow even more. In the eyes of her millions of fans, Adele has proven the old adage to be accurate: absence makes the heart grow fonder. "Sometimes I wonder if I've missed [my chance] by a year. But you know, I was being a mum. I couldn't rush it. And you've got to give people a chance to miss you." The "sabbatical", as Adele calls it, away from the constantly moving juggernaut that is the conventional industry album-tour-album-tour work ethic, came to an end after the birth of her son, Angelo. With Adele claiming her new and chaotic role as a mother inspired her to start

▲ Adele takes centre stage at the 85th Academy Awards ceremony, performing to Hollywood's A-list celebrity elite.

◄ Adele and Paul Epworth hold their 'Skyfall' Oscars tight. The song gave Bond his first Oscar in 47 years.

*"No one wants to listen to a record from someone who has lost touch with reality. I live a low key life for my fans."*

writing and recording music again, in order for her child to "know what I do", the break was also instrumental in throwing off the handcuffs of *21*, shackles that had bound her musical identity so tightly to her past, and to relationships that no longer mattered. "I was very conscious not to make *21* again," she said to *i–D*. "I definitely wasn't going to write a heartbreak record 'cos I'm not heartbroken. How I felt when I wrote *21*, it ain't worth feeling like that again. I was very sad and very lonely. Regardless of being a mum or a girlfriend, I didn't want to feel like that again."

On October 19, 2012, Adele and Simon welcomed Angelo into the world. It was an event that would turn Adele's own world upside down, for the better. "How's life as a mum? It's f**king hard. I thought it would be easy. Everyone f**king does it, how hard can it be?"Adele told *i-D* in November 2015. "It is hard, but it's phenomenal. It's the greatest thing I ever did. Angelo makes me be a d**khead, and he makes me feel young and there's nothing more grounding than a kid kicking off and refusing to do what you're asking of them. It used to be that my own world revolved around me, but now it has to revolve around him." The famously tour-shy singer now has a three-year-old audience-of-one every day, but instead of belting out 'Rolling in the Deep' it's the 'Wheels on the Bus', and instead of sleeping on a tour bus for months on end, she could sing loud and proud in the comfort of her own home. "I felt so mega having given birth; the confidence from that, I felt unstoppable. I'm sure most women feel that." Speaking to *The Guardian* in November 2015, she continued: "Towards the end of *21*, I couldn't remember why I was doing it any more. I couldn't answer the question: 'Why am I halfway around the world? On

my own?' But then, after I had my son, I thought, 'Yeah, that's why I did it all.' I felt proud of what I'd achieved with *21* for the first time. And now everything I do, in every channel of my life, is part of a legacy that I'm making for my child. I want my child to see his mum running a proper business again. Being a boss again. Hopefully smashing it again." And "smashing it" is precisely what Adele has done.

But, not before a few false starts, and recording an entire album worth of songs – which may never see the light of day – that her *21* producer, Rick Rubin, felt simply weren't good enough to release. This setback was a crushing blow to Adele's confidence. It was back to the drawing board. But, as a strange twist of fate would have it, just as the sky was falling down on Adele's run of creative fortune, musical inspiration would return in the shape of a charismatic superspy known as Bond, James Bond, for what turned out to be the most successful Bond film ever, *Skyfall*.

"I was a little hesitant at first to be involved with the theme

▲ Adele and Simon attend the 55th Annual Grammy Awards, Los Angeles, February 10, 2013.

song for *Skyfall*," Adele said in a statement in 2012, released on the James Bond Facebook page. "There's a lot of instant spotlight and pressure when it comes to a Bond song. But I fell in love with the script and Paul Epworth had some great ideas for the track and it ended up being a bit of a no-brainer to do it in the end." In November 2015, days before *25*'s release, Adele made her fans laugh out loud when she admitted in an interview with *i-D* about why she was conspiciously abscent from publicizing the song: "I gave birth a few nights before the *Skyfall* premiere, that's why I didn't do anything for it. He was about to drop out my fanny at, like, any moment!"

The song 'Skyfall' received critical and commercial acclaim and won Adele and Paul Epworth an Academy Award. After the L.A. ceremony on February 26, 2012, in Adele's blasé style, she exclaimed to the world's press, "I haven't decided where to put the Oscar yet. I want it to be somewhere where I'll see it every day. Bathroom, bedroom, yeah, somewhere like that." *Skyfall*'s theme song was the first time a Bond song had won an Oscar in 47 years, and only then it was for *Thunderball's* special visual effects category. This high recognition of the track was incredible considering Adele claimed writing the track took just "two studio sessions". In a statement released on Facebook, Adele said that recording the Bond theme was, "one of the proudest moments of my life. It was also a lot of fun writing to a brief, something I've never done, which made it exciting. I'll be backcombing my hair when I'm 60 telling people I was a Bond girl back in the day, I'm sure." The experience of recording such a successful Bond song has left a sweet Hollywood taste in the singer's mind, "Maybe someday I'll do a musical!" she teased.

With her Oscar in the bag, and Hollywood bowing at her feet, it wasn't long before the Queen of England followed suit, and awarded Adele a Member of the British Empire (MBE) medal, on December 19, 2013. On the day of receiving this prestigious award, from Prince Charles, no less, it was evident that Adele felt like a fish out of water, but beaming from ear-to-ear nonetheless. If you watch her receiving the medal on YouTube, you can see her laughing her now-famous dirty laugh throughout the entire ceremony, as if struck by an intense case of the giggles at just how ridiculous her life was turning out. After the ceremony at Buckingham Palace, Adele posted a statement to her website: "It was an honour to be recognized and a very proud moment to be awarded alongside such wonderful and inspirational people," before adding it was "very posh indeed!" An Oscar and an MBE in the same year. What on earth could happen next?

Following the success of *Skyfall*, Adele choose not to capitalize on her Oscar glory and, again, dove back under the covers to continue recording *21's* long-awaited follow up. For the first time in the singer's recent career, things started to unravel, the new songs were not arriving as she had hoped, the pressure mounting. The writing was on the wall, and Adele was in the fog of writer's block. Things weren't all bad, however, Adele passed her driving test – a highlight of her hiatus period that she is immensely proud: "I still can't believe I can drive actually". But, despite everything at home being glorious, the false starts of following up such an influential record had continued to take their toll, and it wasn't after a meeting

▶ Performing 'Hello' live, for TV show Skavlan, December 3, 2015.

▶ Adele, Jennifer Lawrence, and Emma Stone go for Mexican food at Cosme, New York, November 23, 2015.

with songwriter, and collaborator on *21*, Ryan Tedder, that the writing of *25* started to stall. It was the song 'Remedy', the fifth track on the album, that provided the undoing. "Because 'Remedy' is so great, and I loved singing it so much I got excited, like, 'I'm on a roll!'. But, I weren't on a roll," she admitted to *i-D*. "So I started knocking out some s**t songs. They were good pop songs, but I was just trying to bang them out. I didn't want to think about it.

▲ Adele and Simon watch Lionel Richie's Sunday afternoon set at Glastonbury Festival, June 28, 2015.

And, you know, it got rejected. My manager was like, 'This isn't good enough.' Ouch. Yeah, it knocked my confidence a bit, but I also knew, you know. Then I flew Rick Rubin over, to play him the songs and he was like, 'I don't believe you.' That's my worst fear: people not believing me. So I went back to the drawing board."

It was back (again) at square one that Adele found inspiration, and the courage to write new songs. To start again. To prove she could do it all again. It was only then could she have a breakthrough. Defeated by a series of unworkable songs, Adele did what she does best – she defied the odds. Of the songs which she recorded, but then scrapped, she says: "I would have been embarrassed if I'd got away with that record. I was trying to hurry." It seemed the world would have to wait even longer for a new Adele track.

*"I'm so sorry it took so long but you know, life happened."*

But just when you thought Adele had gone too far over the horizon, viewers of *The X Factor* on October 18, 2015 were treated to a tiny snippet, no more than a few seconds, of a new song. It was called, fittingly, 'Hello'. Its teasing in this way, during an advert break, in front of six million Saturday night TV viewers, not only broke the internet that weekend, but was also undeniable proof that new music was on its way. The song, a haunting ballad with an epic chorus, was also a statement of intent. Before the album's release on November 20, 2015, 'Hello' tore download and CD sales charts, in almost every country, to pieces. "It seemed the right way to start. After my sabbatical." Adele said of her spectacular return. "I think the song is representative of the record, and it's the perfect song to come back with. It's very conversational, which I think is important." Written with Greg Kurstyn, 'Hello' went straight to number one in the UK and US and the accompanying music video, directed by Xavier Dolan, totted up more than 650 million YouTube views in the first three weeks alone. The song broke records everywhere it went.

Within two weeks of 'Hello''s first radio airplay, Adele had released her third album, *25*, and once again, completely defied all

▲ Adele in Soho, New York, on the day of the release of *25*, November 20, 2015. Bodyguard, Peter van der Veen, becomes one of the most photographed men on the planet.

expectations, and allayed all her fears and insecurities. "Turning 25 was a turning point for me, slap bang in the middle of my 20s," Adele said in her first major interview for almost two years. "*25* is about getting to know who I've become without realizing. And I'm so sorry it took so long, but you know, life happened."

"I'm 60 per cent excited. 40 per cent s\*\*tting it!" she said in an November 2015 interview with *Vice*, revealing her vulnerability at how fans could possibly respond negatively to the new material. "'Hello' is about hurting someone's feelings but it's also about trying to stay in touch with myself, which sometimes can be a little bit hard to do and about wanting to be at home and wanting to reach out to everyone I've ever hurt – including myself – and apologize for it."

With the song entrenched at No.1 around the world, and the news that an album was to follow shortly, the world once again went Adele-mad. While writing the album may have been a peak-and-trough process, Adele's central vision for the songs – once they had arrived in her mind and were flowing out of her – remained true since day one of the recording process. "I was never going to write my record about Being Someone Really Famous," she told *The Guardian*, "because who cares? *25* is an album about reaching out to everyone that I've ever loved in any way, shape or form and admitting that I was wrong sometimes."

The album, as with every Adele record, started with a trip to the shops to buy herself a new lyric notebook. "I do it every album. I walk to the shops, I buy a new pad, sniff it – 'cos smell is important," she reveals to *i-D*, "and then I get a big, fat Sharpie pen and write my age on the front page. *25* has five exclamation marks after it 'cos I was like, 'How the f**k did that happen?!' 21 to 25. Though I think this will be my last age one," she reveals to Zane Lowe on Apple Music's Beats1, of the album's numerical title. "I feel like there's been a massive change in me in the last couple of years," she continues. "Having become a parent, and me and all my friends suddenly living grown-up lives and having responsibilities we haven't had before. I feel like how I feel about myself is how I'm going to feel about myself forever. I feel like the idea of naming albums after my age is always to show a photograph of what's going on in my life at that time. I feel like not that much is going to change profoundly in me from now on, in terms of how important years of my life are to myself. I think the next one is probably going to be called *Adele: The Real Me...*I'm just kidding." With 11 complete songs on the record, plus an extra four set aside to potentially be released at a later date, *25* is Adele's most personal, and honest – and fun – album yet. 'Send My Love To Your New Lover', for example, with its calypso-inspired beat is great to boogie too: "It's a bit of fun, innit?" Adele says of the track. "You ain't got to be dark all the time". *25* had taken two years to shape and record. Upon its release, buoyed by the radio airplay of 'Hello', *The Daily Show* host Trevor Noah joked that Adele was solely responsible for climate change, with all of her fans' tears responsible for the rise in global water and flooding. A joke, yes, but one that made clear that Adele's position as the world's most sincere, honest and popular artist was hers and hers alone. No one could touch her. The comeback was complete. The album's themes of nostalgia, regret, yearning for all things past, and motherhood had resonated quite dramatically with her fans and critics alike – Rick Rubin was right all long. As long as Adele stayed true to herself, the fans would stand by her. Selling a record-breaking 3.4 million copies in its first week on sale in the US, and notching up the largest single sales week for an album since records began monitoring sales in 1991, *25* has also become the first album to sell more than three million copies in a week in the US and has shifted more than 800,000 copies in its first week of release in the UK – more copies than the next 86 albums in the charts combined!

With the possibilities for Adele's continuing success a blank page, the singer has recently experienced an increase in her 'advertising reach' and is receiving offers to promote every product under the sun in order to increase her "brand" exposure even more. Everybody, understandably, wants a piece of Adele. But, in typical Adele style, she laughs off any suggestion that she is for sale. "What [adverts] have I said no to? Everything you can imagine. Literally every-f**king-thing. Books, clothes, food ranges, drink ranges, fitness ranges... That's probably the funniest. They wanted me to be the face of a car. It's, like, I don't want to endorse a line of nail varnishes, but thanks for asking!" she wrote in the *Observer Music Magazine*, during her brief tenure as guest editor during the week run-up to *25*'s release. As fans have known for a long time, the lure of fame, wealth and the spotlight is not enough to entice Adele, the princess of the common people, to sell her soul, even if she is also the first to admit that, she is, "... an artist. I have an ego. And it likes to be fed!" But when it comes to fame, Adele's mind is made up: "It's very easy to give in to being famous. It's powerful. It draws you in. Really, it's harder work resisting it. But after a while I just refused to accept a life that was not real."

With the future always just around the corner, a sold-out world tour in support of *25* in 2016, the release of new music and the possibility of acting, Adele's future is burning brighter than ever before. But, as always, the prospect of taking *25* on tour is a daunting one, and brings back unpleasant memories of chronic stage fright, insecurity and loneliness. "There is something quite lonely about going on stage in front of loads of people and then everyone going home," she told the *New York Times*. "Performing to that many people for every night, for that long, I find something very lonely about it. Which sounds weird, because you're performing for like, 20,000 people every night, but you leave on your own. You don't go home and, like, share a bed with 20,000 people and have a little pyjama party and watch movies."

As yet another wave of Adele fever spans across the globe, it is clear that the singer has once again found her voice in fine form and is happier than ever.

> *"It's very easy to give in to being famous. But after a while I just refused to accept a life that was not real."*

"For a while, it felt like this moment was never gonna come 'cos I couldn't access myself to write a record," she told *i-D* on the eve of *25*'s escape. "So I'm super chuffed and really proud of the songs. I'm s\*\*tting myself about it all, but it will be exciting." With world domination in the bag, it is inevitable that our thoughts turn to what happens next for this phenomenal singer, the loveable scamp with that dirty laugh and a love of cursing. "I'd like to tour properly … I'd like to make another record. I'd like to be able to stand the test of time and keep up with the speed that the world is moving. I'd like to make records forever with the time I've been given for this one." This long-term plan will certainly make Adele's fans delirious with happiness, even if they have to wait another four years to hear any new material.

But, as *25* has proven, it'll be well worth the wait...

▶ Adele's new bob haircut makes headline news after her thrilling appearance on the UK's *X Factor* Final, December 13, 2015.

# 7

# Accolades and Adulation

In 2011 and 2012, Adele was not only ruling the radio waves on both sides of the Atlantic, but was also totting up No.1 albums and singles in countries she had not yet visited on tour. In the process of this staggering success, there was one whisper that was silently and doing the rounds at every label in London: Adele had changed the music industry. There was no going back. *21*, an album from which Adele had accumulated much wealth and acclaim, was heralded as "a moon landing", a generational one-off, the likes of which we will not see for another few decades. According to a variety of sources, that album was the most-requested record in karaoke bars, at funerals and on long-haul flights (for nervous flyers). British media even reported that when a mother sang 'Rolling in the Deep' for her daughter, who had been in a week-long coma at Leeds Hospital, the child instantly, and magically, awoke. The power of Adele, it seems, transcends consciousness. Adele was no longer just a BRIT-school scruff from Tottenham – she was pop royalty, a Princess Diana-type for the Founders generation. As recently as August 2015, four years after its initial release, *21* was still being purchased a couple of thousand times a week. To date, *21* has sold more than 30 million copies, placing Adele in the pantheon of all-time music greats, even outselling her musical idols such

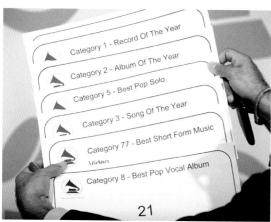

▲ Adele is thrilled by her tally of six awards at the 54th Annual Grammy Awards.

as Lionel Richie and Michael Jackson. Adele's mantelpiece was no longer full of half-filled cups of cold PG Tips. Now, it shone with shining hometown glory as well as an Oscar, an MBE, seven Grammys, two Brits, two Ivor Novellos, three AMAs, two Aims, an Ascap, an Impala, a Mobo, two Music Week awards, two Q awards, four MTV awards, two Nickelodeon awards, a Glamour award, two German Echos, two French NRJs, a Polish Fryderyk, a Mexican Premios Oye! and a Canadian Juno. These awards were had vbecome symbolic of Adele's influence and impact, but also her personal wealth, estimated at around £50 million, with Forbes placing her on top of their prestigious Richest Under 30 list, ahead of One Direction and Calvin Harris.

It was on February 12, 2012 – the night of the 54th Grammy Awards – that 'Adele the Superstar' was born, and she took Simon with her. Nominated for a staggering six statuettes at the ceremony, she hit the red carpet showcasing a new look that caused a flashbulb-popping frenzy. Her long auburn locks were gone and in their place was the curled golden blonde bob of a 1940s Hollywood screen siren. She wore a curve-skimming long black dress and her lips were slicked with vampish red lipstick. It had been four months since she'd last made a public experience and she was back with an oh-so-glamorous bang. Fans, friends, family, and all the artists and industry insiders in the Staples Center in L.A., awaited her first, post-surgery live performance with bated breath – and perhaps just a touch of trepidation. Would her voice hold out? Would it sound as good? The answer was: yes – if not better. Performing a scorching, pitch-perfect version of 'Rolling in the Deep', her voice had never sounded clearer or more powerful. She didn't just look like she belonged at that star-studded L.A. auditorium, she ruled it.

It was a special and unusual night in many ways. The day before the ceremony the sad and shocking news of Whitney Houston's death had broken. The story was all over the news, and as the singer had been due to attend the show, there was an extra element of disbelief. As such, emotions were running high. Grammys host LL Cool J read out a moving prayer for Houston, while Jennifer Hudson paid tribute with a poignant performance. There was also a tribute to Adele's old idol Etta James, who had passed away at the end of 2011. A bittersweet feeling permeated the arena, but despite the circumstances, Adele managed to bring a smile to the faces of everyone there.

Shattering her own expectations, and looking stunned with each announcement, she took home the silverware for the first five categories in which she had been nominated. 'Rolling in the Deep' beat Katy Perry's 'Firework' and Bruno Mars's 'Grenade', amongst others, to the title of Record of the Year. The track also beat 'Grenade' and Mumford & Sons' 'The Cave' to Song of the Year, and Radiohead's 'Lotus Flower' amongst others, to Best Video. In the Best Pop Solo Performance category, 'Someone Like You' beat Lady Gaga's 'You and I', Pink's 'F**kin' Perfect', and Katy Perry's 'Firework'. *21* meanwhile, eclipsed *Born This Way* by Lady Gaga – who incidentally sat in the audience sporting a rather more sombre expression than usual, to match her muted black outfit – *Loud* by Rihanna, *Doo-Wops & Hooligans* by Bruno Mars, and *The Lady Killer* by CeeLo Green for Best Pop Vocal Album. All that was left to take home was the Big One…

Diana Ross came on stage to present the Album of the Year and left a dramatic pause before announcing the winner. The nominees – Adele, Lady Gaga, Rihanna, Bruno Mars and the Foo Fighters – all wore nervous smiles. When Adele's name was called, the crowd roared its approval. For a second, the cockney chanteuse sat stock-still, looking like it was all too much to take in. Perhaps she had just acknowledged that in that second she'd equalled her heroine Beyoncé's 2010 record tally of six awards in one night, or that she had beaten Amy Winehouse's, Lauryn Hill's, and Alicia Keys' tallies of five awards each at the 2008, 1999, and 2002 ceremonies respectively. Or perhaps, she was just genuinely disbelieving. With her hand on her heart and a nervous smile on her face, she turned to Simon for a kiss, before hugging her team. As she walked through the crowd to receive her award, she was wiping her eyes, and by the time she got to the stage she was in the midst of a full-blown sob. "Oh my God, oh my God, thank you", she cooed in her broadest cockney. Then pulling herself together for a moment, she waved her award and shouted, "I firstly want to say, Mum, girl did good! Mum I love you so much." Joined on stage by *21's* producers, she tearfully did her "thank yous" before pausing to wipe her nose and cackle, "Oh my god, a bit of snot!" – which of course, resulted in the audience collapsing into giggles. It was Adele through and through.

It capped an amazing night of TV for her. The Grammys had been prefaced by an exclusive interview with Adele on CBS's long-running *60 Minutes* show in which journalist Anderson Cooper had introduced her by naming 2011 'The year of Adele' – and it didn't sound like hyperbole. The interview took place in Adele's London recording studio and in her new home, a £7m Surrey mansion – which, she explained, offered her some privacy from the notoriously invasive British tabloid press. In typically unguarded fashion, she spilled her heart out on a range of topics, including her current status as the world's most popular singing star. "The level of fame I'm dealing with now was almost overnight. I landed on a flight to New York and was literally the most talked about artist in the world that day," she said, eyes widening. "I thought it was hilarious. It's not really my cup of tea having the whole world know who you are. I find it quite difficult to think there are 20 million people listening to my album, which I wrote quite selfishly to get over a breakup. I didn't write it thinking this was going to be a hit."

She also opened up about Simon – with a twinkle in her big green eyes and a wide smile on her face. Bubbling with excitement, she referenced the 'Someone Like You' lyrics and said, "I have met someone else now and he's much better than him. In fact next time I might sing 'Never mind, I've found someone like you... please forget me.'"

There was more to come. Less than a fortnight later, Adele appeared at the 2013 BRIT Awards. After another scintillating live performance, she was named Best Female Artist and she had her Union Jack-patterned statuette presented to her by Kylie Minogue. As expected, she also bagged the Album of the Year trophy. Although the live ceremony was to end in controversy

after producers cut her acceptance speech off to introduce a performance by Blur (which saw Adele famously flip the bird "at the suits"), the evening nevertheless became another cause for celebration, and once again resulted in a massive sales surge.

Meanwhile, in the States it was announced that Adele had broken Whitney Houston's record – *21* had become the longest-running US chart album in history for a female artist, having spent an entirely apt *21* consecutive weeks at the top. She was to go on to stay at the summit of the *Billboard* charts for an unbroken 23 weeks, and in spring *21* had been certified 8x platinum. Adele was to break even more records: the DVD of her Royal Albert Hall gig, *Live at the Royal Albert Hall*, scored the highest one-week tally for a music DVD in more than four years, going 9x platinum. And when her third US single release, 'Set Fire to the Rain' also shot to the top, Adele became the first artist in history to lead the *Billboard* 200 consecutively, with three *Billboard* Hot 100 number ones. She was also the first female artist to have three singles in the US Top 10 at the same time, and the first female artist to have two albums in the top five of the *Billboard* 200 and two singles in the top five of the *Billboard* Hot 100, simultaneously. She was quite simply, unstoppable. Her triumphs had taken her from international success to global ubiquity.

Not just a modern-day musical icon, Adele also cemented her status as a global style icon when she landed her first US *Vogue* cover in 2012. Looking ethereally gorgeous on the cover of the March issue, she gave an interview that proved no matter how many records she smashed, awards she bagged, or albums she sold, no matter how much she blossomed into a Botticelli-esque beauty, or how many front covers she graced, she would always be the same old loveable, down-to-earth Tottenham girl. She might have Anna Wintour's personal number in her mobile phone these days, but she hasn't affected airs and graces, or started to believe in her own hype. She has not tempered that salty language or censored her ribald sense of humour, either. Showing how completely unfazed she was by her own star status, she grumbled, "I hate the red carpet. I don't feel insecure, I just feel like, 'Oh, I don't want to do this.'"

◀ Hanging out at the 2012 Grammy Awards with Sir Paul McCartney.

Typically open, she talked about her illness and operation, describing how her enforced silence had helped her find a kind of peace and given her space and time to reflect on her achievements – finally allowing herself to feel a little proud. "The noise in my life just stopped. It was like floating in the sea for three weeks. It was brilliant," she said.

It wasn't just the people on the street that were full of praise for this new singing sensation. Adele was beginning to amass fans in celeb world too – a list of A-list fans that could have stretched from Tottenham to London Bridge and back. Whether it's Beyoncé calling her "the best," her hubby Jay-Z agreeing, Kylie saying, "I love her, her music, her story, her humanity, her dirty jokes," or his musical royal highness, Prince, saying, "When she just comes on and sings with a piano player, no gimmicks, it's great." Even Lady Gaga graciously says Adele deserves all that has come her way (even though that means she has less silverware adorning her bedroom shelves these days).

And it's not just those in the music industry who sing Adele's praises, everyone in the world of entertainment seems to have fallen for her, from the producers of *Saturday Night Live*, who introduced a regular 'Someone Like You' skit on the show (in which everyone who hears the song instantly bursts into tears), to acting royalty, such as Julia Roberts, star of one of Adele's favourite childhood films, *Notting Hill*. Roberts said, "Adele's music is so personal that you get invested in her life. When Adele had her health scare, I had random people saying to me, 'Oh my God, did you hear about Adele?' We feel like Adele's in our book club or she lives in our neighbourhood – that's a gift, to make people feel that way." Roberts had hit the nail on the head.

Adele's music is utterly inclusive, connecting with people across the globe and across the spectrum, and her success – not least because she emerged in a digital age of social networking, music file sharing and illegal downloading – is unprecedented. Her albums look set to keep smashing records, too – everyone relates to having their heart broken, after all. With *21* and *25* continuing to shift huge units, her future doesn't just look bright, it looks bright enough to make you reach for your shades. Naturally the crew at her label XL

▲ Adele, emotional and overcome, and backed by her famous producers whilst accepting a Grammy Award at the 2012 bash.

are beyond thrilled and excited about what the future holds. But then they were always confident that their girl had the potential to shake the music industry to its foundations. "The whole message [with Adele] is that it's just music, it's just really good music. There is nothing else. There are no gimmicks, no selling of sexuality," XL founder Richard Russell told *The Guardian*. In never resorting to a raunchy promo vid or sexed-up live show, Adele, he believes, has not only been a burst of fresh air for audiences, she has also altered the pop landscape for future female artists. "I think in the American market, particularly, they have come to the conclusion that is what you have to do. Now you see that Adele is No.1. What a great thing, how amazing. Not only are young girls going to see that, but the business people who are behind all those videos. It's going to make them rethink what they should be doing," he said.

Adele's high-profile bevy of production pals are hugely proud of her march to superstardom, too, and are in no doubt why she is such a phenomenon. Speaking to the *NME*, Paul Epworth said it was down to her unwavering honesty. "She's a true artist. She writes with integrity from the heart. She's brave for sharing her experiences through her songs. She's done something really soulful and connected with people in an age of artifice." Rick Rubin is on the same page, describing her as "the real thing," the joyful antithesis to manufactured pop music, and capable of bringing tears to grown men's eyes. He doesn't think the world has even seen the best of her yet. "There are a ton of places Adele can go, I don't think we have even touched the surface of where she can go creatively," he told *M* magazine. "Can we replicate the phenomenal sales of *21* on every record she releases? Probably not, but I honestly believe Adele is an artist that will have a 30- or 40-year career."

Her fans love that she is no puppet too, they love that she pulls her own strings. Her decision to stay with independent record label XL – with none of the obligations, time constraints and pressures of a major – attest to that. She's never had to sell her sexuality, she hasn't slimmed down to a waif because a man in a suit or a glossy magazine told her to (she's slimmed down naturally as a result of her own decision to give up drinking and take up Pilates, actually, and she has even quit smoking). She's never felt the need to turn down the volume on her voice, or censor herself. She sets herself apart from other artists by not courting the paparazzi or allowing her private life to be speculated upon. She spurns the spotlight and lets her music do the talking – of course, the killer detail being that while she keeps her life private, her music is heart-on-the-sleeve revealing.

Still so young, Adele is only at the beginning of her journey, and despite the jokey threats of disappearing into obscurity to grow a vegetable patch, she knows she's in it for the long haul – which is a scintillating prospect for her fans and all those around her. "I want to evolve as an artist. There's so much music I don't know about yet. I want to go on the road with my friends who are artists. I want to go and see things as a fan again. I am a fan, but I can't remember what it feels like to be a fan anymore. Because I've become an artist," she has said. '*The*' artist, you could say. It's always been about the music for Adele, but she has no ruthless master plan. "I see no appeal in having a very specific plan as an artist. Who f\*\*king cares if people

don't get it or don't like it? I'd rather trust myself, to like what I've done and stick to my guns than make music I don't like, wear clothes that don't suit me and flutter between genres because I'm scared I won't be relevant if I pass my 'sell-by' date," she has said.

And that's what we love about her. Adele is a rare gem in the often contrived, manufactured and cynical world of pop music. From her heart-breaking voice to her unguarded chatter, her revealing lyrics, right down to her filthy laugh, she has proved that by being yourself you really can have it all.

▲ Record-breaking, attention-demanding, soul-stirring Adele is a modern icon in every sense of the word.

*"I find it quite difficult to think there are 20 million people listening to my album, which I wrote quite selfishly to get over a breakup. I didn't write it thinking this was going to be a hit."*

BRIT
AWARDS
2012
with
MasterCard
Peter Blake
WELCOME
WELCOME

# Discography

## Singles

### 2007
'Hometown Glory'

### 2008
'Chasing Pavements'
'Cold Shoulder'
'Make You Feel My Love'
'Hometown Glory'

### 2010
'Rolling in the Deep'

### 2011
'Someone Like You'
'Set Fire to the Rain'

### 2012
'Rumour Has It'

### 2015
'Hello'

### 2016
'When We Were Young'

## Albums

### 2008
*19*

### 2011
*21*

### 2015
*25*

# Picture Credits

The publishers would like to thank the following sources for their kind permission to reproduce the pictures in the book.

Corbis/Tom Wallace/Minneapolis Star Tribune, 2. Getty Images/Jeff Kravitz/FilmMagic, 4. Getty Images/Dave M. Benett, 7. & 8. Contour by Getty Images, 11, 14-15, 19, 22-23 & 24. James Davies, 27. Alamy/Adrian Lourie, 28. Getty Images/Samir Hussein, 31. Camera Press/Chris McAndrew, 32. Corbis Outline/Ben Rayner, 33. Camera Press/Suki Dhanda, 35. Camera Press/Chris McAndrew, 38-39. Corbis Outline/Ben Rayner, 40. Camera Press/Chris McAndrew, 42. Corbis Outline/Ben Rayner, 43. Corbis Outline/Dan Burn-Forti, 44-45. & 46. Getty Images/ Dave Etheridge-Barnes, 49. Getty Images/Michael Burnell, 50-51. Rex Features/Brian Rasic, 55. Camera Press, 56. Alamy/AlamyCelebrity, 57. Getty Images/Michael Loccisano, 58. Rex Features, 59. Rex Features/David Fisher, 60. Getty Images/Dave Hogan, 61. Rex Features, 62. Getty Images/Gareth Davies, 63. Camera Press/Michael Clement, 65. Camera Press/Dean Chalkley, 66. Photoshot/Edd Westmacott/Retna, 67. Corbis, 69. Camera Press/Dean Chalkley, 70. Getty Images/Jay West/WireImage, 71. Getty Images/Astrid Stawlarz, 73. Getty Images/NBC Universal, 74-75. Getty Images/Jeff Kravitz/FilmMagic, 76.Getty Images/Ed Rode, 79. Photoshot/Edd Westmacott/Retna, 80. Getty Images/Jeff Vespa/WireImage, 81. Getty Images/Pxl8/WireImage, 82. & 83. Photoshot/Robin Francois/Retna, 84-85. Getty Images/Jeff Kravitz/WireImage, 87. Corbis Outline/Jason Joyce, 88. (top) Rex Features/Elma Okic, 88. (bottom) Rex Features/Eric C. Pendzich, 91. Corbis Outline/Samuel Kirszenbaum, 92. & 94-95 Contour by Getty Images, 98. Getty Images/Mike Coppola/FilmMagic, 100-101. Camera Press/Suki Dhanda, 103. Corbis/Larry Hirshowitz, 104. (top) Corbis/Chad Bukta, 104. (bottom) Getty Images/Mark Venema, 107. Getty Images/NBC Universal, 108-109, 111 & 113. Contour by Getty Images, 114-115. Getty Images/Andy Sheppard/Redferns, 117. & 119. Contour by Getty Images, 120. (top) Rex Features/Jim Smeal/BEI, 120. (bottom) Getty Images/Andy Sheppard/Redferns, 122-123. Getty Images/Jon Furniss/WireImage, 124. Getty Images/Dave Kotinsky/Wireimage, 126-127. Corbis/Tom Wallace/Minneapolis Star Tribune, 129. Getty Images/Dave Hogan, 130-131. Getty Images/Matt Kent/WireImage, 132. Rex Features/Tom Dymond, 135. Getty Images/Stefan M. Prager/Redferns, 137. Getty Images/NBC Universal, 136. Rex Features, 141. & 142. Getty Images/Kevin Mazur/WireImage, 144-145. Getty Images/Stefan M. Prager/Redferns, 147. Rex Features, 149. Syco/Thames/Corbis, 150. (top) Robert Gauthier/Los Angeles Times via Getty Images, (bottom) Jeffrey Mayer/WireImage/Getty Images, 152. Lester Cohen/WireImage/Getty Images, 153. John Stillwell - WPA Pool/Getty Images, 155 (top) REX/Shutterstock, (bottom left) Josiah Kamau/BuzzFoto via Getty Images, (bottom right) Jason Bryant/LNP/REX Shutterstock, 157. Raymond Hall/GC Images/Getty Images, 161. Syco/Thames/Corbis, , 163. (top) Corbis/Armando Arorizo, (bottom) Getty Images/Frederic J. Brown/AFP , 167. Robert Gauthier/Los Angeles Times via Getty Images, 168. Larry Busacca/Getty Images For The Recording Academy, 171. Obyn Beck/AFP/Getty Images, 173. Jon Furniss/WireImage/Getty Images, 174. Gareth Cattermole/Getty Images

Every effort has been made to acknowledge correctly and contact the source and/or copyright holder of each picture and Carlton Books Limited apologizes for any unintentional errors or omissions, which will be corrected in future editions of this book.